THE BEAN TREES

Barbara Kingsolver

TECHNICAL DIRECTOR Maxwell Krohn
EDITORIAL DIRECTOR Justin Kestler
MANAGING EDITOR Ben Florman

SERIES EDITORS Boomie Aglietti, Justin Kestler
PRODUCTION Christian Lorentzen

WRITER Laurel Rayburn
EDITORS Emma Chastain, John Crowther

This edition published by Spark Publishing

Spark Publishing
A Division of SparkNotes LLC
120 Fifth Avenue, 8th Floor
New York, NY 10011

02 03 04 05 SN 9 8 7 6 5 4 3 2 1

Please send all comments and questions or report errors to
feedback@sparknotes.com.

Library of Congress information available upon request

Printed and bound in the United States

RRD-C

ISBN 1-58663-473-9

INTRODUCTION: STOPPING TO BUY SPARKNOTES ON A SNOWY EVENING

Whose words these are you *think* you know.
Your paper's due tomorrow, though;
We're glad to see you stopping here
To get some help before you go.

Lost your course? You'll find it here.
Face tests and essays without fear.
Between the words, good grades at stake:
Get great results throughout the year.

Once school bells caused your heart to quake
As teachers circled each mistake.
Use SparkNotes and no longer weep,
Ace every single test you take.

Yes, books are lovely, dark, and deep,
But only what you grasp you keep,
With hours to go before you sleep,
With hours to go before you sleep.

CONTENTS

CONTEXT

BARBARA KINGSOLVER WAS BORN in 1955. She was raised in a part of eastern Kentucky positioned between extravagant horse farms and impoverished coalfields. Although rich imagery of her home state fills many of her novels, Kingsolver never imagined staying in the region. She left Kentucky to attend to attend De Pauw University in Indiana. Kingsolver majored in biology in college and took one creative writing course.

Kingsolver became active in anti-Vietnam protests during her college years, which marked the beginning of her commitment to political and social activism. A few years after her graduation, she went to the University of Arizona in Tucson, where she earned a masters of science degree in biology and ecology. Kingsolver supported herself working at a variety of jobs until she finished graduate school, at which time she got a job as a science writer for the University of Arizona. This job led her into journalistic writing. Her numerous feature stories have appeared in many nationally acclaimed publications. According to Kingsolver, journalism and scientific writing helped her develop good discipline and paved the way for her career in fiction writing.

In 1985, Kingsolver married. After becoming pregnant, she began struggling with insomnia. Her doctor suggested that she scrub the bathroom tiles with a toothbrush to tire herself out. Instead, Kingsolver spent her sleepless nights curled up in a closet writing her first novel, *The Bean Trees*. *The Bean Trees* was an immediate success among book critics when it was published in 1988, but more important to Kingsolver, it was also widely read by people from all walks of life. Kingsolver has firmly committed herself to keeping her work accessible; while she hopes that literary types will appreciate her writing, she also wants to know that people in rural Kentucky read and enjoy her novels.

Kingsolver believes in writing that promotes social change. She is committed to social and environmental causes, and *The Bean Trees* reflects this commitment. Kingsolver's dedication to literature with a social conscience led her to found the Bellwether Prize for Fiction, which was awarded for the first time in 2000. She continues to work as an environmental and human-rights activist.

Kingsolver's background in ecology and commitment to activism are evident in *The Bean Trees*, but she resists further conjecture about her life's influence on her work. Although her readers are often eager to assume her work is autobiographical, the author claims that only small details come directly from her life experiences; the rest is invented.

Since her first novel, Kingsolver's work has continued to meet with success. *Pigs in Heaven* (1993) is the popular sequel to *The Bean Trees*. Her other novels include *Animal Dreams,* (1990) *The Poisonwood Bible,* (1998) which was an Oprah Book Club selection and earned international praise, and *Prodigal Summer.*

Plot Overview

Tне ВЕАN ΤREES opens in rural Kentucky. The novel's protagonist, Taylor Greer, who is known at the beginning of the novel by her given name, Marietta, or by her nickname, Missy, remembers a moment in her childhood when Newt Hardbine's father was thrown to the top of the Chevron sign after his tractor tire exploded. Ever since then, Taylor has been afraid of tires. Taylor goes on to tell the story of Newt Hardbine, a peer of Taylor's who died while Taylor was still in high school. Although Newt and Taylor seemed like identical kids when they were small, Taylor was the one to escape small-town life. She did so by avoiding pregnancy, getting a job working at the hospital, and saving up enough money to buy herself an old Volkswagon bug. About five years after high school graduation, Taylor says goodbye to her beloved mother, Alice Greer, and leaves Pittman County, Kentucky, for good.

The protagonist decides that she will drive until her car runs out of gas and then take a new name based on wherever she is when her car stops. She ends up in Taylorville, and changes her name from Marietta to Taylor. Her car breaks down in the middle of the Cherokee Nation in Oklahoma, and she stops in an old bar for a cup of coffee and a hamburger. As she sits in her car, getting ready to leave, a woman approaches and puts a baby in the front seat of Taylor's car, telling her to take it. She tells Taylor she is the sister of the child's mother and that the baby was born in a Plymouth car. The woman leaves with no further explanation. Taylor is bewildered, but drives off with the child. They go to a hotel, and while bathing the baby, Taylor discovers that the baby, a girl, has been abused and sexually molested. She names the baby Turtle because the girl clings to things like a mud turtle.

Eventually, Taylor and Turtle make it to Tucson, Arizona. When Taylor's two back tires blow out, Taylor goes to an auto-repair shop called Jesus Is Lord Used Tires. There she meets the owner, a kind, wise woman named Mattie. Mattie takes to Turtle right away. Taylor moves into a Tucson hotel with Turtle and finds a job working at the Burger Derby.

The narrative switches to the story of Lou Ann Ruiz, another Kentuckian living in Tucson. Lou Ann has been abandoned by her husband, Angel. On January 1, she gives birth to a son, Dwayne Ray. Lou Ann's mother and Granny Logan come west to visit the baby, and Granny Logan brings water from the Tug Fork River in Kentucky, which she suggests should be used to baptize the baby. When Angel comes home to gather up some of his things, he pours the water down the drain.

Meanwhile, Taylor has started her new job, but she quits six days later. She begins to look for a place to live, and finds a room for rent listed in the paper. The room turns out to belong to Lou Ann. The two women become fast friends, and Taylor takes the room. Without work, Taylor is left with no option but to take a job working for Mattie at Jesus Is Lord Used Tires. One day Taylor meets two of Mattie's friends, Estevan and Esperanza, a married couple from Guatemala. Soon, it is evident that they are illegal aliens living with other illegal aliens in Mattie's home above the tire shop.

A month or so later, Taylor takes Turtle to see a doctor and finds that Turtle's growth has been stunted because she was abused. Turtle is not a baby, as her size indicates, but a three-year-old. That same day, Angel tells Lou Ann that he is leaving her for good.

Mattie's friend Esperanza attempts suicide. When Estevan comes to tell Taylor this news, he ends up divulging the story of their past. He tells her that he and Esperanza had to leave behind a child in Guatemala. The government wanted the names of union members from Estevan and Esperanza and took their daughter, Ismene, as a way of forcing them to tell. Choosing to save seventeen lives instead of trying to get their daughter back, the couple fled their country. Estevan spends the night on Taylor's couch. Taylor realizes she is falling in love with him.

After a few weeks, Lou Ann gets a job at a salsa factory, supporting herself in the absence of her husband. No sooner does she start her new job than Angel sends a package with presents for Lou Ann and Dwayne Ray, and a letter asking her to come live with him in Montana, or, if she does not want to do that, to let him come back and live with her in Tucson. After consideration, Lou Ann refuses to take him back.

On the night of the first summer rain, Mattie takes Esperanza, Estevan, and Taylor into the desert to see the natural world come to life. Turtle is left with her baby-sitter, a blind woman named Edna Poppy. Edna and Turtle go to the park, and because of her disability, Edna does not notice when a prowler approaches Turtle. Taylor returns and hears as much of the story as Edna can tell: Edna heard struggling and swung in the direction of the attacker with her cane. She hit him and then felt Turtle tugging on the hem of her skirt. Turtle does not seem hurt, but she has stopped speaking and has the same vacuous look in her eyes that she had when Taylor first saw her. Turtle's trauma and the difficulties of Estevan and Esperanza make Taylor depressed. To make matters worse, the police investigation into the attack on Turtle reveals that Taylor has no legal claim on Turtle. Taylor will be forced to give her to a state ward or find a way around the law. The social worker in Tucson gives Taylor the name of a legal advisor in Oklahoma, where the laws are different.

Mattie becomes worried about Estevan and Esperanza's safety. A recent crackdown on illegal immigration will force them to find a new home and a way of getting there. Taylor decides she will transport Estevan and Esperanza to another sanctuary for illegal immigrants in Oklahoma. While there, she will look for Turtle's relatives and see if they will consent to a legal adoption. Once in Oklahoma, Taylor returns to the bar where she received Turtle but finds that it has changed owners. There are no signs of the people she met there seven months before. Taylor, Esperanza, and Estevan decide to go to the Lake o' the Cherokees. During that time, Taylor concocts a plan to convince the authorities in Oklahoma that Estevan and Esperanza are Turtle's biological parents.

Once in the office of Mr. Armistead, the legal authority in Oklahoma, Esperanza and Estevan pretend to be Turtle's biological parents. Esperanza sobs real tears at the prospect of giving up Turtle, and Taylor realizes that Esperanza is grieving the loss of her own daughter, who looked so much like Turtle. Taylor and Turtle drop off Esperanza and Estevan at their new home, a church in Oklahoma. Taylor says a tearful goodbye to Estevan. Taylor then calls her mother, who comforts her. Taylor and Turtle head back to Tucson, a place that both of them now call home.

CHARACTER LIST

Taylor Greer The protagonist of the novel, Taylor also narrates much of the story. She is a strong, gutsy woman, and her voice is both sassy and kind. Born and raised in rural Kentucky, she leaves to escape a small life in her hometown. Like her mother, she is proud of her Cherokee blood.

Turtle The child given to Taylor in the middle of the Cherokee nation. She gets her name from her clinginess, which reminds Taylor of the mud turtles in Kentucky. She is so quiet and unengaged that many believe her to be dumb or retarded. This silence, however, is due to Turtle's history: although she is only three years old, Turtle has already been physically and sexually abused. Although Taylor has spent her life avoiding pregnancy, she keeps Turtle with her.

Lou Ann Ruiz A Kentuckian woman who settled in Tucson with her baby, Dwayne Ray. Her husband, Angel, has just walked out on her when the story begins, and Taylor and Turtle move in with her. She worries about the terrible accidents and horror stories she hears about, fearing for the safety of herself and her baby. More sensitive and more provincial than Taylor, she is nonetheless a survivor.

Mattie The owner of Jesus Is Lord Used Tires and a mother figure for Taylor. She is wise and kind. She allows illegal immigrants to stay in her home, operating a kind of sanctuary. Her garden of beautiful vegetables and car parts is an inspiration for Turtle, whose first word is *bean* and who loves all kinds of vegetables.

Estevan   A Guatemalan refugee, he worked as an English teacher in Guatemala before he and his wife fled to the United States. He speaks beautiful English, and his kind ways inspire romantic feelings in Taylor. He lives in Mattie's building with his wife, Esperanza. He enlightens Taylor about the corruption of Central American governments.

Esperanza Estevan's wife. Her grave demeanor is a reflection of her sorrowful past. Turtle's presence touches her because Turtle reminds her of the daughter she had to leave behind.

Ismene   Estevan and Esperanza's daughter, whom they left in Guatemala. She represents both the horror of political corruption and the desperation that can necessitate the abandonment of children.

Angel Ruiz Lou Ann's husband, he is a Mexican man whom Lou Ann met when he worked in the rodeo in Kentucky. Angel's prosthetic leg—the result of a pickup truck accident—wounds his pride terribly and makes him unhappy.

Alice Greer Taylor's mother, who lives in Kentucky. In Chapter One, Taylor says that her mother expects the best from her daughter and thinks that whatever Taylor does is wonderful. An encouraging, kind mother, she is the only part of Taylor's hometown that Taylor misses when she leaves.

Dwayne Ray Lou Ann's son. He was born on New Year's Day.

Newt Hardbine A classmate of Taylor's. He drops out before graduation to help his family on its farm and dies before Taylor leaves Pittman County. He represents what could have been Taylor's fate had she not had a wonderful mother and the determination to leave town.

Mrs. Virgie Parsons Lou Ann's grumpy neighbor, who
      sometimes baby-sits for the children. She makes
      insensitive remarks about immigrants.

Edna Poppy The blind woman who lives with Mrs. Parsons. She is
      much warmer than her roommate.

Cynthia The social worker who comes over after Turtle's run-in
      with a miscreant in the park. Her prim attitude annoys
      Taylor, but her intentions are good.

Mr. Jonas Wilford Armistead The legal authority in
      Oklahoma City who oversees Turtle's adoption. An
      old white man, he treats Esperanza and Estevan like
      ignorant foreigners.

Granny Logan Lou Ann's grandmother. She is provincial and
      harbors many prejudices about Angel's nationality. She
      hates the arid climate in Tucson and brings Lou Ann
      water from the Tug Fork River in Kentucky so that she
      may baptize Dwayne Ray properly.

Ivy Lou Ann's mother. She fights perpetually with Granny
      Logan, her mother-in-law. Like Granny Logan, she is
      provincial and has no interest in seeing Arizona.

Mrs. Hoge and Irene The mother and daughter, respectively,
      who run the Broken Arrow Motor Lodge, where
      they let Turtle and Taylor stay free of charge on their
      trip west.

Father William The priest who works with Mattie, transporting
      illegal immigrants to and from her house.

Lee-Sing The woman who owns the grocery store and
      Laundromat next door to Jesus Is Lord Used Tires. Her
      mother brought the original bean seeds from China,
      the descendents of which now grow in Mattie's yard.

ANALYSIS OF MAJOR CHARACTERS

TAYLOR GREER

Taylor Greer is gutsy and practical. She views her hometown as stifling and tiny, and she decides she wants to avoid the trap of an early pregnancy and make her escape to a more interesting life. Taylor's spirited, quirky voice shapes the novel. She perceives things in an original fashion, communicating her wonder at the customs and landscape of the Southwest with unusual metaphors and folksy language. Taylor settles in Tucson, Arizona, because its landscape strikes her as outlandish; newness and amusement appeal to her more than comfort or familiarity. As she contends with dangerous poverty, an unasked-for child, and many other trials, Taylor's wit and spirit remain intact.

Although never naïve, Taylor becomes even more worldly after learning about the political corruption and personal tragedy faced by Estevan and Esperanza and the abuse inflicted on Turtle. Her sympathetic reaction to the difficulties of others reveals Taylor's tenderheartedness. Taylor cares for the abandoned and the exiled with increasing enthusiasm as the novel progresses. Mattie calls her a hero for risking her own safety in order to achieve a more just society. In some ways, Taylor is an archetypal hero: she leaves her home and family, descends into darkness, and reemerges to accomplish some good for the sake of her society. She also functions as Esperanza's comedic counterpart. Whereas tragedy permanently enshrouds Esperanza's life, Taylor has a chance to hold on to her daughter and her happiness. Unlike traditional female heroines, Taylor's adventures do not revolve around finding or keeping a man. Her life focuses instead on females—primarily on Turtle, but also on her mother, her friend, and her mentor. The male-female love she experiences remains purely platonic.

LOU ANN

Lou Ann is soft, motherly, and worrisome; she fears her own death and the death of her child. Far more womanly in a traditional sense than Taylor is, she pines for her husband and expresses her conviction that marriages and love should last forever. A Kentuckian, she retains the innocence of a small-town girl. Despite this innocence and occasional spates of homesickness, Lou Ann demonstrates her grit by moving to Tucson and then staying there alone to raise a child over the objections of her female relatives. She and Taylor form a functional family, caring for their children and for each other.

Lou Ann undergoes a transformation from dependent housewife into strong single mother. She has feminist instincts from the beginning of the novel, but initially she does not express them. She remains silent even though the sight of the local strip joint makes her shudder; she notices that her house feels more whole with her female relatives present than with her husband; she reflects on the strength of her body during her pregnancy. Around Chapter Ten, Lou Ann changes. She begins to speak about the contradictions and injustices of gender relations. She tells Taylor that she despises the obscene painting on the door of the strip joint. She searches for a job and accepts that she will have to support herself. She acts more boldly, scolding Taylor when Taylor does not fight hard for her rights.

ESTEVAN

Though a cast of strong women peoples *The Bean Trees*, the only male character of consequence is Estevan, whose presence grows more important as the novel progresses. Taylor's affection for him suggests that he is a welcome addition to an otherwise exclusively female world. Estevan represents the opposite of the stereotypically chauvinistic American male. A good man, he counters the novel's villainous and sexually predatory men, such as Turtle's abuser, the prowler in the park, and the absentee Angel. We empathize with Estevan not only because of his kindness, but because he lacks a homeland. Like women and like the natural environment, he knows destruction and persecution. Via Estevan, Kingsolver dispels many myths about illegal immigrants. One myth holds that immigrants cannot speak English well, but Estevan speaks better English than any of the native English-speakers in the novel. His pristine English and impeccable grammar suggest his intelligence and industry.

TURTLE

A history of abuse makes Turtle silent for much of the novel. She seems almost catatonic, anxious to remain unnoticed and therefore unmolested. However, as the novel progresses and Turtle begins to trust that Taylor will take good care of her, the three-year-old girl becomes increasingly talkative and charming. She begins to preface friends' names with the word *Ma*: Lou Ann becomes Ma Woo-Ahn, for example. She demonstrates a connection with the earth, taking great pleasure in naming vegetables and playing with seeds or dirt. Her made-up songs concern vegetables, and her preferred bedtime story is the seed catalogue. This love of the land links her, Kingsolver suggests, to her Native American heritage.

ALICE GREER

One of the first characters we meet, Alice Greer sets the precedent for the series of strong, loving women that come after her in the novel. Kingsolver suggests that children become what they are told they will become; because Newt Hardbine is told he will fail, for example, he does fail. In contrast, because Alice constantly tells Taylor she is wonderful and smart and will succeed, Taylor is wonderful and smart and successful. Alice also represents the independence from men advocated by the novel. She lives happily, sometimes married, sometimes not, and never imagines she needs a man in order to raise Taylor.

MATTIE

Mattie acts as a mother to hundreds of people, including Taylor. She does not fit the typical portrait of a mother figure, however, for although she is wise and loving, she is also fearsomely intelligent and tough. Her combination safe house, garden, and tire shop symbolize Mattie's combination of qualities. Mattie does not push anyone to act heroically, as she herself acts, but she does inspire heroism through her own actions. She also breathes fresh air into the lives of her provincial, undereducated friends with her work as an intellectual. The other characters only dimly grasp her work as an activist and an intellectual, but the fact that it exists points to a world outside the novel's scope.

Themes, Motifs & Symbols

Themes

Themes are the fundamental and often universal ideas explored in a literary work.

The Shared Burden of Womanhood

The topic of gender is explored in two general ways in the novel. First, the novel shows the success of a nearly exclusively female world. Taylor lives in a small community of women who for the most part live their lives independently of men. The women in this community strengthen one another. Once she begins to share her life with Taylor, Lou Ann stops disregarding her appearance, finds a job, and forgets her irresponsible husband. Taylor, the once-invulnerable spirit, finds the energy to fight for Turtle only after weeks of Lou Ann's prodding and a long talk with Mattie. The women are remarkably loyal to one another. When she sees Esperanza's tearful catharsis, Taylor realizes that if Esperanza asked for Turtle, Taylor would give Turtle to her. Esperanza's loyalty to Taylor is equally strong, for although Turtle is one of the only things that gives Esperanza joy, Esperanza does not ask Taylor to give up Turtle.

Second, the novel portrays gender inequality as a societal phenomenon instead of as a series of individual grievances. When Taylor first sees Turtle's body, she says that the burden of being born a woman had already affected the little girl. This comment immediately suggests that Kingsolver does not mean for us to think of Turtle as an individual but as representative of women in general, all of whom face difficulties because of their gender. Women suffer because they are women. Men touch and prod Lou Ann when she takes the bus, and the strip joint with its lewd paintings offends her. Esperanza seems to have had fewer educational and occupational opportunities in Guatemala that her husband did. While Estevan can speak perfect English, she is isolated in her depression, unable to express her grief fluently.

THE PLIGHT OF ILLEGAL IMMIGRANTS

Kingsolver makes it clear that she sympathizes with the plight of illegal immigrants. Mattie, one of the most beloved characters in the novel, transports and protects illegal aliens. The immigrants Estevan and Esperanza are depicted sympathetically, and Taylor's horror at their past life changes the way she sees the world. Kingsolver depicts those who denigrate immigrants not as evil, but as ignorant or misguided. Virgie Parsons's views represent politically conservative ideas about immigration and nationalism. Although her remarks seem insensitive to Taylor, Virgie is not depicted as an evil person, but instead as one who has latched on to a political ideology without considering its moral implications.

Kingsolver also breaks down the us-versus-them rhetoric that often surrounds immigration issues by likening Taylor to Esperanza and Estevan. She levels the hierarchy that values an American citizen over a Guatemalan immigrant by depicting Taylor and the married couple as refugees. Taylor not only describes herself as an alien in Tucson, she finds that she is an outsider in the Cherokee nation, where Esperanza and Estevan feel at home.

RESPECT FOR THE ENVIRONMENT

The novel expresses a concern for the environment not by focusing on the potential destruction of the environment, but by focusing on the beauty of the land. The novel also suggests that Native American heritage and respect for the environment go hand in hand. Chapter Twelve dramatizes the intimate relationship between the land and indigenous peoples when Taylor, Esperanza, Estevan, and Mattie reenact the celebration of the first rainfall; we learn that as a child, Taylor loved to climb trees, behavior her mother ascribed to Taylor's Cherokee inclination get high up in a tree to find God; Taylor's sudden need to see Lake o' the Cherokees has to do with her Cherokee blood; and Turtle has a natural love for the earth. Finally, the way that Turtle and other displaced people are symbolized by birds makes a statement about the vulnerability that Native people share with nature: both birds and displaced people will be hunted down if they cannot find a sanctuary.

MOTIFS

Motifs are recurring structures, contrasts, or literary devices that can help to develop and inform the text's major themes.

REBIRTH

The pattern of death and new life is repeated throughout the novel. Often, this motif is associated with dualities: when one member of a pair dies, the other gains life force. Newt Hardbine is represented as a kind of double for Taylor: in grade school, people could hardly tell them apart, and their lives seemed to move in parallel directions until they became older. Newt's death at the beginning of the novel can be viewed as a sacrifice that allows Taylor to get away. His death functions as a kind of symbolic sacrifice that allows his counterpart to prosper. In a similar way, when Taylor leaves her hometown, Alice Greer stops being her daughter's caretaker, and Taylor starts being Turtle's caretaker. Only after she separates herself from her mother does Taylor come upon Turtle in the Oklahoma bar. Turtle's reenactment of her mother's burial symbolically allows Taylor to take over as mother. Esperanza's cathartic experience—pretending that Turtle is her daughter and pretending to give her away—symbolically lays Ismene to rest, so that Turtle, Ismene's double, may live and thrive.

Turtle embodies the novel's rebirth motif, undergoing a series of metaphoric deaths and resurrections. When Taylor first finds her, Taylor does not know if Turtle is dead or alive. Gradually, Turtle shows signs of life, as her abuse becomes a more distant memory and she learns to trust Taylor. This cycle goes another round when Turtle is attacked in the park, returns to her catatonic state, and then learns to trust again. Taylor's fascination with seeds and vegetables represents her reenactment of the cycle of burial and new life. The dried-up seed that, once buried, becomes a living thing, symbolizes her own life experience.

MOTHERHOOD

The Bean Trees explores several models of mothering, none of them conventional. Taylor, Lou Ann, and Esperanza make up a trio of mothers, and none of them fits the stereotypical model of motherhood. After avoiding pregnancy her whole life, Taylor is given an Indian child; Lou Ann's husband abandons her before her child is born; Esperanza must leave her child in order to save the lives of others. All three of these mothers love their children fiercely. They also place their love for children above their love for men: Taylor restrains her impulse to initiate an affair with Estevan (which Estevan does not want either) because she identifies with Esperanza as a mother and does not want to worsen the pain Esperanza feels at having lost a child.

Kingsolver suggests it is unrealistic to expect perfection from mothers. She depicts Esperanza's decision to abandon her child as painful but also understandable and even noble. She does not blame Taylor when Turtle is left with a blind baby-sitter and attacked by an assailant. Kingsolver values the attempt at responsible parenting over the results.

SYMBOLS

Symbols are objects, characters, figures, or colors used to represent abstract ideas or concepts.

BEANS AND BEAN TREES

"Bean," Turtle's first word, symbolizes the promise that, like a dried-up seed that grows, a mistreated woman may thrive if given enough care. The bean trees, another name for the wisteria vine that Turtle spots in Dog Doo Park, symbolize transformation, a spot of life in the midst of barrenness. The bean trees have a symbiotic relationship with bugs called rhizobia, which move up and down the wisteria vine's roots and provide a network that transfers nutrients. This mutual aid symbolizes the help and love human beings give one another. The bean trees, like people, only thrive with a network of support.

ISMENE

Ismene symbolizes all abandoned children, and the grief of all mothers forced to abandon them. Since we never meet her in the narrative and only hear about what she means to her parents, to Taylor, and to Turtle, Ismene is nothing but a symbol in the novel. She exists as Turtle's dark twin, the embodiment of what could have happened to the abandoned Turtle had not Taylor rescued her. Ismene reveals Kingsolver's commitment to writing as a means of social change, for Kingsolver portrays Ismene as representative of the pain inflicted by political corruption.

BIRDS

Most often, birds are metaphorically associated with Turtle, the abandoned child with strong survival instincts. As Turtle's life changes, so do the birds that symbolize her. Taylor makes her first sound, a quiet laugh, when the car she is in stops to allow a mother quail and her babies to pass. Turtle is beginning to feel safe in the small family composed of herself and Taylor, and so the birds that elicit a happy sound from her are a mother quail and her chicks. Later, Taylor takes Turtle to the doctor and discovers the gravity of the abuse Turtle has suffered. As she makes this discovery, she sees a bird outside the doctor's window. The bird has made its nest in a cactus. Like the bird in the cactus, Turtle's life persists in spite of her painful surroundings. After Turtle encounters the prowler, a sparrow gets caught in Lou Ann's house, and the bird's fear suggests Turtle's own fright and confusion. The sparrow's survival suggests that Turtle will survive.

SYMBOLS

SUMMARY & ANALYSIS

CHAPTER ONE: THE ONE TO GET AWAY

SUMMARY

The narrator begins by recounting events in her adolescence, when she lived in Pittman County in rural Kentucky and was known as Missy. Since then, she has changed her name to Taylor. (To avoid confusion, she is referred to as Taylor throughout this summary.) Taylor tells the story of Newt Hardbine's father, who was inflating his tractor tire when it overfilled and exploded, throwing him to the top of a Chevron sign. The accident left him deaf. Taylor explains that she and Newt Hardbine look like brother and sister. Like the Hardbines, Taylor and her mother are poor. Taylor says that no one could predict whether she or Newt would be the one to "get away."

Taylor continues to attend high school, and Newt drops out to work on his father's tobacco field. He impregnates a girl named Jolene Shanks and marries her. Many girls at the high school drop out to have babies, but Taylor makes up her mind to avoid pregnancy. She credits her handsome science teacher Mr. Hughes Walter for changing her life, since he tells his class of a "real job" working at Pittman County Hospital. With her mother's encouragement, Taylor applies for the job and gets it.

One day, when Taylor is working at the hospital, Jolene and Newt are brought into the emergency room. Jolene's shoulder is bleeding from a bullet wound, and Newt is dead. From clues and insinuations, we gather that years of abuse and neglect from his father led Newt to shoot Jolene and himself. The horror of the scene makes Taylor vomit. Later that night she decides she will not quit her job, since she has survived the worst she will see.

With the money Taylor earns from her job, she buys a rundown '55 Volkswagen bug and decides to leave Pittman for good. Her mother realizes that Taylor wants to leave and makes her daughter prove that she can change the car tires and tend to the car if it breaks down. As she drives off, Taylor (who at this point still goes by the name Missy) promises herself that she will change her name by driving until the gas runs out and naming herself after whatever town she happens to land in. She ends up calling herself Taylor because she runs out of gas in Taylorville. She also promises herself to drive west until her car dies and then settle wherever she ends up. She breaks the second promise when the bug dies on the Great Plains of Oklahoma, a vast expanse that depresses Taylor with its flatness.

Taylor's car breaks down in the Cherokee Nation in Oklahoma. Taylor and her mother have "head rights"—that is, they have enough Cherokee blood that they are permitted to live in the Cherokee Nation if they choose. Taylor finds the Nation disappointing. Exhausted, she stops in a bar for some coffee. She picks out a postcard decorated with a picture of two Indian women on it, one of whom is wearing red and turquoise, Taylor's favorite colors. At the bar sit an Indian man and a mean-looking white cowboy. An Indian woman sits at a table, looking cautiously at the men. When Taylor gets into her car to leave, the woman follows her and sets a baby down in the passenger seat, telling her to take it. She says only that the baby belongs to her dead sister and that Taylor should not go back into the bar. Then she walks away, leaving the baby with Taylor.

Taylor starts driving. She cannot determine the child's gender, and it keeps so quiet that Taylor wonders whether it is alive or dead. When Taylor realizes the child has wet itself, she stops at a motel, where she persuades the kind woman working at the front desk to let them stay free of charge. In the motel room, Taylor gives the child a bath and sees that it is a girl and that she has been bruised and sex-ually abused. Taylor, shocked, almost throws up. She puts the baby to bed and writes a postcard to her mother, saying, "I found my head rights, Mama. They're coming with me."

ANALYSIS

The first chapter introduces us to the strong idiosyncratic voice of Taylor Greer. She uses slangy Southern language and describes the world in off-kilter metaphors. She also uses hyperbole and narrates in a gently sarcastic tone. A dependable narrator, she establishes our trust in her storytelling. The first chapter introduces one of the novel's central ideas: the importance of motherhood. Kingsolver contrasts the effect of Alice Greer's good parenting with that of Mr. Hardbine's and Mr. Shanks's bad parenting, suggesting that parents determine their children's destinies. Because Alice constantly tells Taylor how wonderful and smart she is, Taylor becomes wonderful and smart. Because Mr. Hardbine abuses his son, his son kills himself. Because Mr. Shanks tells Jolene she is a slut, Jolene gets pregnant. Jolene acknowledges the direct effect of parents' words on children's behavior when she says, "[M]y daddy'd been calling me a slut practically since I was thirteen, so why the hell not? Newt was just who it happened to be."

Taylor makes herself literally homeless when she leaves Kentucky, and she feels figuratively homeless when she reaches the Cherokee Nation. She had thought of the Nation as her ace-in-the-hole, her homeland, but to her dismay, she finds it depressing. She thinks Oklahoma and the Nation so disheartening that she breaks her own promise to herself, and instead of settling where she lands she spends most of her savings to get her car fixed so she can leave. By the end of the chapter, however, Taylor begins to rethink her own definition of home. She had associated the idea of home with a physical place, thinking of Kentucky or the Cherokee Nation as her homeland, but when she writes to her mother and says she will take her head rights (meaning the baby) with her, it suggests that Taylor is beginning to think of home as a connection with people rather than as a place.

Beginning in this chapter, Kingsolver portrays women as oppressed and mistreated. In Taylor's hometown, pregnancy is depicted as a disease that spreads to most of the girls, a disease to be avoided with determination and luck. When Taylor sees that the baby has been sexually abused, she remarks that the baby's gender "has already burdened her short life," which suggests her belief that sooner or later, all women are burdened as the girl has been. The fact that Taylor immediately characterizes this specific instance of sexual abuse as a universal female experience rather than an isolated perversion suggests that Taylor and the novel itself regard women as besieged. The discovery of the abuse inflicted on the baby solidifies Taylor's commitment to the young child. At first she does not know what to do with the child, but immediately after seeing proof of sexual abuse, Taylor writes her mother to say that her "head rights . . . [are] coming with [her]," implying that she now sees the child as an inalienable part of her.

CHAPTERS TWO–THREE

SUMMARY—CHAPTER TWO: NEW YEAR'S PIG

The narrative voice shifts from Taylor to that of an anonymous, omniscient narrator who introduces us to Lou Ann Ruiz, a Kentuckian living in Tucson, Arizona. Lou Ann is pregnant, and as the chapter opens, her husband, Angel, has just left her. Three years earlier, Angel lost the lower half of his leg in a car accident. When Lou Ann got pregnant, she stopped having sex with him. Convinced that his amputation repulsed Lou Ann, Angel accused her of wanting to sleep with other people. Lou Ann feels that Angel no longer likes her or anyone else.

The narrator describes Halloween, the day on which Angel leaves Lou Ann. Lou Ann goes to the doctor and, while in the waiting room, hopes that her child will not be born on Christmas. She has negative associations with the day, since Angel lost his leg on Christmas. Moreover, she does not want her baby to feel robbed of his own special birthday, which he might if it fell on a holiday. The doctor informs Lou Ann that she must lose weight. She takes the bus home, enjoying the novelty of personal space. Because of her pregnancy, men no longer make suggestive remarks or brush up against her. She gets off the bus and walks past Jesus Is Lord Used Tires, a store featuring a large painted mural of Jesus with a tire dangling below him. Next to the tire store is Fanny Heaven, a nightclub and pornography shop. Lou Ann stops at Lee Sing Market to buy diet food. Lee Sing, the owner, predicts Lou Ann will have a girl. Lee Sing says having a girl is like feeding the neighbor's New Year pig—all your care goes into something that will end up with another family. Offended, Lou Ann thinks that even though she proved Lee Sing right by leaving her native Kentucky, her brother also left.

At home, Lou Ann realizes that Angel has left her. She observes what he left behind and what he took with him, and she thinks that his choices reveal more about him than she learned in nearly five years of marriage. He took beer mugs, a picture of himself at the rodeo, and the television, but he left behind all the kitchen things and sheets and blankets. Children come to her door and for a moment frighten her until she remembers it is Halloween. When Lou Ann goes to bed, her feet are so swollen she cannot get her shoes off. She weeps.

SUMMARY—CHAPTER THREE: JESUS IS LORD USED TIRES

Taylor stays through Christmas at the hotel in Oklahoma, helping Mrs. Hoge with the chores and earning a little money. She has named the baby Turtle because of its firm grip. Around New Year's Day, Taylor and Turtle leave the hotel and start driving. When they reach Arizona, the topography and sky seem so surreal to Taylor that she decides to stay there. It begins to hail, and Taylor pulls off the highway in Tucson. A man points out that she has two flat tires. A few blocks down the road, Taylor finds Jesus Is Lord Used Tires. There she meets Mattie, the kind older woman who runs the place. Mattie tells Taylor that Taylor's two back tires are shot. Taylor cannot afford new ones. To cheer up Taylor, Mattie invites her and Turtle inside and gives Taylor coffee and Turtle apple juice and crackers. Mattie drinks from a mug decorated with pictures of rabbits having sex, and Taylor puzzles over this lack of prudery in someone who owns a shop called Jesus Is Lord Used Tires. Mattie explains that she and her late husband opened the place and that he was a fanatical Christian. A priest stops by. An Indian family sits in his station wagon. He seems nervous and leaves quickly.

Taylor marvels at Mattie, this woman who understands cars and runs her own business, and thinks that in her hometown such a woman would be scorned and ignored. Mattie takes Taylor and Turtle out to the back of the house, where they see her amazing and unusual garden, which is filled with flowers, vegetables, and car parts, including an entire Thunderbird minus the wheels. Mattie shows Taylor her purple beans, the seeds of which she received from the Chinese woman next door, who vows they are descendants of seeds she brought from China in 1907.

Tucson feels like a foreign country to Taylor, and the city seems years ahead of Kentucky. She and Turtle stay in the cheap Hotel Republic downtown. One day she ventures into a museum filled with modern, nonrepresentational sculptures made of sand. Another day, she asks about a job at the hospital, but she is turned away. She meets a friendly woman named Sandi who works at Burger Derby and has a baby boy. Sandi loves the Kentucky Derby, and it thrills her that Taylor comes from Kentucky.

ANALYSIS — CHAPTERS TWO–THREE

In Chapter Two, the narrator allows us a glimpse into the thoughts of one character, Lou Ann, but does not reveal the thoughts of any other characters. This type of narration can be labeled either limited omniscient or subjective. The chapter begins with the narrator informing us that Lou Ann comes from Kentucky. This fact gives us an immediate reason to identify Lou Ann with Taylor, who also comes from Kentucky. As the chapter continues, however, the narrator's presentation of Lou Ann's character reveals that Lou Ann differs markedly from Taylor. Unlike Taylor, Lou Ann worries incessantly. She worries about Angel, she worries that her baby will be born on Christmas day, and she worries about the truth of Lee Sing's axiom about girls.

The narrator presents Angel as a wounded, proud man, asking us to simultaneously understand his insecurity about his leg and hurt pride over Lou Ann's refusal to sleep with him, and to condemn his abandonment of the pregnant Lou Ann. Angel weakens Lou Ann. When she argues with him, she feels "her bones were made of . . . the rubber in a Gumby doll." Still, Lou Ann emerges from this chapter as a character with some backbone. In fact, her greatest moment of power comes when she ventures out by herself. She enjoys the fact that men leave her in peace because of her pregnancy. On the bus, she relaxes, feeling as if she has a "magic circle" around her that no one can penetrate.

Taylor's reaction to Tucson demonstrates her unique way of perceiving the world. To Taylor, a Kentuckian who has left her home county for the first time, Arizona seems so surreal that it makes her laugh aloud. The similes that Taylor uses to describe the land and sky make the images clear, but they also communicate the unique way Taylor takes in her surroundings. She describes the pink clouds as "hippo ballerinas in a Disney movie" and compares the rock structures to mating potato bugs and dinosaur droppings. Taylor's reaction to this place allows us to see a different side of her character. The novel has already established her grit and sense of humor, and here it establishes her sense of adventure. It becomes clear that Taylor heads west not to find beauty, but to find something strange and interesting.

Taylor gently pokes fun at religion. The names Jesus Is Lord Used Tires and 1-800-THE-LORD tickle Taylor because they use God to sell commercial products. Another mild subversion of religion is Mattie's garden, reminiscent of a topsy-turvy Garden of Eden. In the biblical Garden, man, woman, and beast grew alongside one another. In Mattie's garden, car parts, or man-made artifacts, exist alongside God's creations, the flowers and vegetables. Mattie's garden also reaffirms the importance of setting. Only in Tucson, Kingsolver suggests, could purple beans and tomatoes grow out of an old Thunderbird in the middle of January.

CHAPTER FOUR: TUG FORK WATER

SUMMARY

Lou Ann's paternal Grandmother Logan and mother, Ivy, have come from Kentucky to visit Lou Ann and her new baby, Dwayne Ray, who was born on the first of January. Angel has agreed to move back in until the mother and grandmother leave in order to keep up an appearance of marital happiness. Granny Logan keeps the curtains shut all the time, saying that hot weather in January will harm the baby. Lou Ann asks her mother if Granny Logan always lived with Lou Ann's mother and father. Her mother tells her that Granny Logan didn't live with them, *they* lived with *her*. Lou Ann's mother says she never wanted to move out and get a place alone with her husband, because she would have been frightened being alone.

Granny Logan complains about the heat in Tucson and accuses Lou Ann of putting on airs. From her purse, she pulls a Coke bottle filled with cloudy water. It is water from the Tug Fork River, where Lou Ann was baptized, and Granny instructs Lou Ann to baptize Dwayne Ray with it. The two older women depart for Kentucky, and Lou Ann imagines going back to Kentucky with them, sitting on the bus between the two constantly feuding women. On the way home from the bus stop, Lou Ann stops to buy some tomatoes from Bobby Bingo. Lou Ann surprises herself by telling him Angel has left her. She thinks about how she kept up a false appearance all week for her mother and grandmother and finds it hard to believe she divulged her secret to a man she hardly knows. At home again, Lou Ann nurses Dwayne Ray and tries to remember her own baptism. Angel comes home, and when Lou Ann smells beer on his breath, she thinks of all the places he frequents of which she knows nothing. He picks up a few of his things. When he sees the bottle of Tug Fork water in the bathroom, Angel asks Lou Ann what it is and then pours it down the drain after hearing that it is Kentucky water for Dwayne Ray's baptism.

ANALYSIS

Chapter Four dramatizes Lou Ann's desire to both live in familiar surroundings with her family and to live with the absent Angel. Lou Ann's mother and grandmother annoy her, but she feels sad to see them go. Angel has left her, and she feels tempted to fall back on her provincial, comfortable childhood. Still, she recognizes that she has become more sophisticated than her relatives, who call Angel a heathen because he is Mexican and express no interest in seeing Arizona. Although the presence of Granny Logan and Ivy comforts Lou Ann, she realizes that she cannot live with them again. She decides to stay in Tucson, and this choice represents a commitment to experiencing the world and living independently. Her decision to stay in Tucson represents one of many similarities Lou Ann shares with Taylor. Like Taylor, Lou Ann finds herself suddenly alone with a child, committed to staying out of Kentucky and sentimental about the mother she loves and honors.

In this chapter, Kingsolver underscores the solidity of the bonds between women. Lou Ann's grandmother and mother annoy, nag, and criticize her, but they are a more reliable presence in her life than Angel is. When Angel returns to the house, the narrator says, "it struck her that his presence was different from the feeling of a woman filling up the house. He could be there, or not, and it hardly made any difference." This indifference about a man's presence echoes Ivy's words; Ivy tells Lou Ann that she would have felt all alone had she moved out of her mother-in-law's house. When Lou Ann points out that she wouldn't have been alone, but with her husband, Ivy reacts as if she had never thought of her husband as company. To Ivy, the companionship of a quarrelsome, grumpy mother-in-law means more than the companionship of a man.

The Tug Fork water becomes associated with Lou Ann, symbolizing her connection to her family. When Granny Logan pulls it out of her bag, she conjures up an image of Lou Ann's baptism. Baptism implies an initiation into a community, a sign that one belongs to a family of people. The presence of the baptismal water and Lou Ann's recollection of her baptism suggest a symbolic renewal of her membership into a community of women.

CHAPTERS FIVE–SIX

SUMMARY—CHAPTER FIVE: HARMONIOUS SPACE

After meeting Sandi at Burger Derby, Taylor gets a job there. While they work, Taylor and Sandi leave their children at the free baby-sitting service the mall provides for mall patrons, and they take turns checking on the kids to make it look as if they are shopping. After only six days of working at the Burger Derby, Taylor quarrels with her boss and gets fired. Worried about her dwindling funds, Taylor looks through the papers for people advertising a room for rent and finds two promising ads. The first place she visits belongs to three new-age hippies named Fei, La-Isha, and Timothy. La-Isha lectures Taylor on the dangers of hot dogs after hearing that Turtle eats them, and Fei explains that the house is a soy-milk collective and each household member must spend seven hours a week straining curd. Taylor goes to the second listing, which turns out to be Lou Ann's house. Within minutes of meeting, the two women are laughing hysterically about the soy-milk collective crowd. They talk easily about their Kentucky origins and their children. Taylor tells Lou Ann the story of Turtle, and Lou Ann introduces Dwayne Ray. When Taylor asks if she can move in, Lou Ann is overjoyed. Lou Ann tells Taylor she worried that Taylor and Turtle were too smart and cute for her and Dwayne Ray, who just scrape by. Taylor tells Lou Ann to stop thinking that everyone is better than she is, saying, "I'm just a plain hillbilly from East Jesus Nowhere with this adopted child that everybody keeps on telling me is dumb as a box of rocks." At this speech, Lou Ann smiles and says happily that Taylor talks just like she does.

CHAPTER SIX: VALENTINE'S DAY

The first frost comes to Tucson on Valentine's Day, and Mattie's beans freeze. Mattie wants Taylor to work at Jesus Is Lord Used Tires, and although Taylor loves Mattie, witnessing the accident that killed Newt Hardbine's father left her with a fear of tires. Finally, she agrees to work for Mattie. As part of the deal, Mattie gives Taylor two free back tires for her car. One day, Taylor confesses her fear, and Mattie calms Taylor a little by explaining that tire explosions are relative to their size and that tractor tires explode more dramatically than the car tires her store services. Lou Ann watches Turtle and Dwayne Ray while Taylor works. Taylor learns that many Spanish-speaking people live with Mattie. Mattie likens her house to a sanctuary, and when Taylor says she has heard of bird sanctuaries, Mattie says her house is similar, but it is for people.

Taylor, in a bad mood, realizes she dislikes the idea that she and Lou Ann are acting like an old married couple—Taylor goes to work, and Lou Ann cooks and takes care of the kids. Over a beer, Taylor asks Lou Ann to stop doing her favors. The two women keep drinking and talking, and after a while Lou Ann realizes she is drunk. She tells Taylor that she never drinks for fear of doing something awful in front of her friends. Once, she and Angel and another couple went out to the desert to look at shooting stars. Lou Ann got drunk. The next day, Angel asked if she remembered the meteor shower they had seen, and she didn't remember it. She worries that Angel left her because she got drunk that night. Taylor says that perhaps Angel was trying to trick Lou Ann and the meteor shower never existed, a possibility Lou Ann never considered. Taylor tells Lou Ann her philosophy about men, which she picked up from instructions on installing a toilet part. The instructions on the package said, "Parts are included for all installations, but no installation requires all of the parts." Taylor does not believe a man exists who could use all the parts of her personality. Lou Ann howls with laughter. The two women stay up, laughing and talking, and Lou Ann tells Taylor that if something was bothering Angel, he would never stay up late with her just to eat and talk together.

Analysis — Chapters Five–Six

Fei, La-Isha, and Timothy strike Taylor as both ludicrous and enjoyable. Their solemnity makes her feel like a naughty child. When she hears that living in the house involves straining curd for seven hours a week, she thinks to herself, "Flaming nurd. Raining turds." Taylor seems to come from a different world than the one these three people inhabit, a contrast that makes Taylor's similarity to Lou Ann all the more striking and comforting. Taylor and Lou Ann inhabit precisely the same world, one of Kentucky roots and single motherhood. Taylor and Lou Ann's meeting seems inevitable and perfect, much like an updated version of the meeting of two star-crossed lovers in traditional romantic fiction. The fact that Taylor finds Lou Ann through an ad in the newspaper implies that fate brought them together, and by alternating chapters, focusing first on Taylor and then on Lou Ann, Kingsolver has built up our expectations that eventually the two women will meet.

In Chapter Six, Mattie acts as a positive presence in Taylor's life. The description of Mattie's garden suggests that beauty can come from ugliness. Although frost has killed the garden, something good comes of it: Mattie picks the green tomatoes so that the frost would not get them, and she makes delicious green-tomato pies. Mattie continues to be a mother figure to Taylor. Just as Taylor's mother, Alice Greer, pushed Taylor to work at the hospital and insisted that Taylor understand cars before leaving home, Mattie pushes Taylor to work at the tire shop and insists that Taylor understand her own fear of tires so that she can overcome it.

Whereas in Chapter Five Kingsolver emphasizes the similarities between Taylor and Lou Ann, in Chapter Six she begins to draw attention to their differences. Taylor does not worry much, but Lou Ann collects newspaper stories about freak disasters and then worries that one of them will befall her loved ones. Taylor can leave Turtle all day without fear, but Lou Ann must watch over her baby at all times. Still, their differences in some ways make them a good match, which makes Taylor's sudden disapproval of their agreement surprising. Because Taylor has no real reason to reject the mutually beneficial relationship she has with Lou Ann, Kingsolver may be suggesting that Taylor's real problem is a fear of attachment. She is growing close to Lou Ann, and it scares her.

The female characters continue to think badly of men. Taylor correctly assumes the worst about Angel. Regarding herself, she asserts that no man can ever fully appreciate her. Lou Ann expresses confidence in men, but Kingsolver portrays this confidence as misguided and naïve, in contrast to Taylor's smart cynicism. After Taylor explains her theory of male inadequacy to Lou Ann, Lou Ann admits that Angel never would have stayed up late with her, talking and eating. Kingsolver portrays this willingness to value female interaction over male-female interaction as a positive step for Lou Ann.

CHAPTER SEVEN: HOW THEY EAT IN HEAVEN

SUMMARY

In March, Mattie, Lou Ann, Dwayne Ray, Taylor, and Turtle go on a picnic near a beautiful creek. Two of Mattie's friends, Esperanza and Estevan, go with them. Esperanza and Estevan are a married couple from Guatemala City. Estevan, who taught English there, speaks better English than any of the American characters do. Esperanza keeps staring at Turtle, and Estevan explains to Taylor that Turtle reminds Esperanza of a child they knew in Guatemala. Estevan and Taylor take a swim in the ice-cold creek water. On the way home, they have to slam on the brakes to make way for a family of quail. Taylor gets teary-eyed at the sight of the bird family. Lou Ann thinks that Angel, instead of being touched, would have wondered how many birds he could hit. Turtle reacts to the sudden stop by doing a somersault and making her first sound: laughter. Taylor feels relieved that Turtle's first sound was a laugh; it reassures Taylor that she is doing a decent job of raising Turtle, for she feels that if Turtle were unhappy, she would not laugh. A little later, as Turtle and Taylor help Mattie plant the garden, Turtle says her first word: "bean."

One night, Lou Ann tells Taylor about her fear that the horrible things she imagines will happen in real life. She tells Taylor that in high school she stood looking over a cliff and imagined jumping. After imagining it, she became terrified that she actually would jump. She says she used to worry that she would say something rude in the middle of church. Taylor says she has felt similarly, and Lou Ann feels relieved that someone understands her.

That night, Edna Poppy and Mrs. Virgie Parsons, two elderly neighbors, come to Lou Ann's house for dinner and to watch Mattie, who is scheduled to appear on TV. Esperanza and Estevan also come over. On television, Mattie talks about human rights, the United Nations, the concept of asylum, and the violence visited upon immigrants who are forced to return to their countries of origin. Edna and Virgie do not understand Mattie's remarks, and neither does Taylor.

Mrs. Parsons assumes that Turtle is Esperanza and Estevan's child, and calls her a naked wild Indian. Estevan, who works washing dishes at a Chinese restaurant, has brought chopsticks to eat dinner with, but Mrs. Parsons turns up her nose at them. She goes on to remark that immigrants should "stay put in their own dirt" and not take American jobs. Turtle tries to put a piece of pineapple in her mouth with her chopsticks, but cannot. To make her feel better and to chasten Mrs. Parsons, Estevan tells a story. He says that in hell, people sit around a big table with plenty of food, starving to death because they must eat with long-handled spoons and cannot manage to get the spoons in their mouths. Heaven, he says, looks just the same: same table, same food, same spoons. But in heaven, the people use the long-handled spoons to feed one another. Estevan demonstrates by feeding Turtle a new piece of pineapple.

ANALYSIS

Turtle's first sound coincides with the appearance of the quail family, birds that suggest several symbolic meanings. Throughout the novel, Kingsolver uses birds to symbolize Turtle. In this instance, just as the baby birds come close to getting killed but survive, Turtle miraculously survives her tortured babyhood. Turtle's little yelp might indicate her recognition of kindred spirits in the birds. The birds also have a symbolic meaning for Taylor. The car squeals to a stop to save the lives of the birds, just as Taylor's life stopped, or changed course, so she could save Turtle's life. Finally, the fact that the car stops for a family of quail suggests that Taylor, Lou Ann, and the others are becoming more and more like a family.

With Estevan, Kingsolver introduces a new kind of male character in her novel. Estevan, unlike the other male characters, is not selfish, abusive, irresponsible, or mean. Rather, he is kind, intelligent, and responsible. Lou Ann draws our attention to this difference when she notes that Angel would have tried to run over the baby birds. In contrast to Angel's cruelty, Estevan slams on the brakes to save them.

Chapter Seven makes explicit Mattie's role as an activist for illegal immigrants and refugees. Clues from previous chapters hinted at her work: Spanish-speaking people constantly staying in her house, a hurried priest with an Indian family waiting in his car, Mattie's explanation to Taylor that she operates a human sanctuary. It now becomes clear to us that Mattie not only works for immigrants' rights, she hides illegal immigrants in her house. The novel takes a political stance, portraying Mattie's work as good and heroic. Edna and Virgie do not understand Mattie's remarks, perhaps deliberately: Virgie harbors very conservative views on immigrants and twists Mattie's ideas in order to hear what she wants to hear. Neither does Taylor fully comprehend what Mattie says, a failure that Kingsolver does not excuse. Because Kingsolver makes the nature and nobility of Mattie's work clear to the reader, Taylor's failure to grasp it seems perplexing and possibly willful. Kingsolver lets us wonder if Taylor *decides* not to understand because the topic scares or upsets her. Estevan's story of heaven and hell continues this political commentary. As he tells the story, he glowers at Virgie, conveying his disapproval of her views on immigrants. She thinks immigrants should fend for themselves and Americans should not help them, just as the hell-dwellers in Estevan's story think only of helping themselves.

CHAPTERS EIGHT–NINE

SUMMARY—CHAPTER EIGHT:
THE MIRACLE OF DOG DOO PARK

"I have always thought you had a wonderful way with words," he said. "You don't need to go fishing for big words in the dictionary. You are poetic, mi'ija." (See QUOTATIONS, p. 51)

Taylor and Lou Ann sit with Turtle and Dwayne Ray in Roosevelt Park, which the local kids call Dog Doo Park. Much to her dismay, Taylor has just found out that her mother plans to marry Harland Elleston, who works at a paint and body store. Lou Ann tells Taylor she should feel good that her mother has enough life in her to marry again, and she accuses Taylor of disliking men. Taylor disagrees, thinking longingly of Estevan. Lou Ann reminisces about her excitement when she first met Angel. The wisteria vines in the park that once seemed dead now bloom a beautiful purple, and Taylor relates them to a biblical story about water pouring out of a rock. Turtle sits in the dirt saying the names of vegetables. Edna Poppy and Mrs. Parsons walk by, and Taylor jokes with Edna, who is wearing all red, as she always does. Mrs. Parsons mentions that Angel stopped by Lou Ann's house this morning while Lou Ann was out. When Taylor asks, Lou Ann says that if Angel wanted to, she would let him move back in.

One day, Taylor tries to apologize to Estevan for Mrs. Parson's rude comments about immigrants. He says that she is like most Americans, who think that if something bad happens to someone, that person deserves it. Taylor and Estevan compliment each other's speech: Taylor loves Estevan's impeccable English, and he thinks her Kentucky accent and expressions are poetic.

Taylor slowly begins to understand what Mattie meant when she called her shop a sanctuary. People come and go often and quietly, and Mattie frequently leaves for days at a time, "going birdwatching"—that is, looking for people who need a safe place to hide.

Taylor decides to take Turtle to the doctor on account of her history of abuse. When the nurse assumes Taylor is Turtle's foster mother, Taylor does not correct her assumption. Dr. Pelinowsky determines that Turtle stopped growing as a result of her abuse, a condition called "failure to thrive." He shows Taylor x-rays of Turtle's compound fractures and says that although he assumed Turtle was two years old, the x-rays indicate that she is actually three. When Taylor protests that Turtle has been growing of late, he assures her that failure to thrive is a reversible condition. While he talks, Taylor looks out the window into the garden, where a bird has made a nest in a cactus.

After they go to the doctor, Taylor and Turtle meet Lou Ann at the zoo. Taylor learns that Angel came back to tell Lou Ann he is leaving for good to join a rodeo on the Colorado-Montana circuit. Lou Ann accuses Taylor of taking Angel's side, but Taylor explains that if she criticizes Angel now, Lou Ann will resent her if Angel ever returns. Over the course of their conversation, Taylor refers to the month of April. Turtle looks up quickly, and the women realize that Turtle's real name is April.

Summary — Chapter Nine: Ismene

Esperanza attempts suicide by swallowing a bottle of aspirin, and Estevan comes to tell Taylor the news. While Mattie takes Esperanza to a clinic, Taylor keeps Estevan company in her house. Taylor realizes that in times of crisis, she "fall[s] back on good solid female traditions," and she tells Estevan she will either keep feeding him or keep talking. He tells her to talk. They sit next to each other on the couch and talk, and Taylor feels terribly attracted to Estevan. She tells a story about a classmate, Scotty Richey, who electrocuted himself on his sixteenth birthday. She explains the cliques at her high school. At the top of the social ladder came the town kids, then the motorcycle crowd, then the farm kids (her group), who were called Nutters because they earned money by picking walnuts. Taylor says that even the Nutters had one another, but Scotty did not fit in anywhere. Suddenly, she gets angry at Esperanza, who, unlike Scotty, had someone, but nevertheless tried to kill herself.

Estevan talks about torture techniques used in Guatemala. He tells Taylor that the police use telephones to shock sensitive body parts with electricity. Estevan implies that Taylor has chosen to ignore these horrors, and she defends herself, saying she does not approve of America's policies and often feels like a foreigner in Tucson, coming as she does from a place were "they use dirt for decoration and the national pastime is having babies." Estevan tells her she does not know what Esperanza has lived through. He tells Taylor that he and Esperanza had a daughter named Ismene, who was taken in a raid on their old neighborhood. Estevan's and Esperanza's membership in the teacher's union made them targets, because they knew twenty people in the union and the government wanted the names of those people. The government wanted to keep them alive since they had valuable information, so it took Ismene to bait Esperanza and Estevan into handing over the names. Esperanza and Estevan chose saving their fellow union members' lives over getting their daughter back, and they fled to the United States. Estevan says that captured children such as Ismene get adopted by families who can afford to care for them—military or government couples. Taylor cries.

Turtle wakes up and joins them. Taylor sees herself, Turtle, Estevan, and the cat, and thinks about a family of paper dolls she had when she was little. She says she longed for the family the dolls had, which was so far beyond her grasp. She thinks that if the world were different, the four of them on the sofa could be the perfect Family of Dolls. Turtle goes back to bed, and Taylor and Estevan sleep on the couch. Estevan and Taylor curl up together in their sleep, but when Taylor wakes and thinks of all Esperanza has suffered, she kisses Estevan's hand and goes to her own bed alone.

ANALYSIS—CHAPTERS EIGHT–NINE

In Chapter Eight, the motif of beauty springing from ugly places recurs. The chapter title, "The Miracle of Dog Doo Park," refers to the blooming wisteria, which appears dead but one day sprouts beautiful flowers. Taylor remarks that the miracle satisfies her even more than the biblical story about water springing from a rock. The story she refers to takes place in the desert when God enables Moses to draw water from a rock to save the Israelites. Taylor and Lou Ann, like the Israelites, find themselves in the desert. Their miracle provides them not with the physical sustenance of water, however, but with the spiritual sustenance of beauty.

Lou Ann and Taylor continue to think of men in different ways. Lou Ann accuses Taylor of thinking "man was only put on this earth to keep urinals from going to waste," and Taylor cannot come up with a man she respects other than Estevan. In contrast, Lou Ann demonstrates her traditional mindset about men and marriage. She flutters with excitement at the thought of Taylor's mother's impending marriage, and when asked if she would take Angel back, responds, "What else could I do? He's my husband, isn't he?"

In several ways, Taylor grows up in Chapter Nine. She finds out about the horror of Esperanza and Estevan's past; she admits to herself her feelings for Estevan; she begins to think about men more objectively; she understands that compared to Esperanza, who has been through so much with her husband, she has no claim on Estevan.

Hearing the horrors of Estevan's past creates a crisis for Taylor. For the first time, she truly comprehends the capacity for cruelty in the world. It seems as if we are meant to agree at least partially with Estevan's idea that Taylor has *chosen* not to understand the horrors in other countries. We have seen in previous chapters that Taylor can ignore what it might pain her to understand. At the same time, her spirited self-defense rings true. She might be ignorant, but she has a good heart and can identify with the refugees' feeling of being lost.

At the same time that Taylor admits that she is attracted to Estevan, she begins to think about men less cynically. For the first time, she expresses a longing for a conventional, nuclear family. When she thinks of her Family of Dolls and sees herself on the couch with a man and child, the idea of a traditional family appeals to her. The fact that Taylor chooses to leave Estevan and go to her own bed demonstrates her strong character. It also demonstrates, perhaps, her new respect for Estevan's family. Estevan already has a real version of the family Taylor imagines for herself, and she does not want to intrude on that. Also, Taylor recognizes Esperanza's claim as wife and mother. When Taylor learns how Esperanza lost her child, she immediately responds and acts loyally to Esperanza partly because of their common bond of motherhood. We see the intensity of Taylor's sympathy for Esperanza when she imagines Esperanza's pain made into a burning pile, centered around a child who looks like Turtle. The power of this vision makes Taylor get up and leave Estevan.

CHAPTERS TEN–ELEVEN

SUMMARY — CHAPTER TEN: THE BEAN TREES

> *Turtle shook her head. "Bean trees," she said, as*
> *plainly as if she had been thinking about it all day. . . .*
> *It was another miracle. The flower trees were turning*
> *into bean trees.* (See QUOTATIONS, p. 52)

The morning after Esperanza's suicide attempt, Taylor feels more optimistic. She hears birds singing and talks with Lou Ann about their calls. The house where she and Lou Ann live is becoming more like a household composed of two women and their children and less like a space Angel left behind. Lou Ann returns from a reunion with the Ruizes, Angel's family. She happily recounts that Angel's entire family, including his mother, thinks him the meanest of the bunch. It seems they still consider Lou Ann part of their family. Lou Ann and Taylor take the children to Roosevelt Park. They sit under the wisteria arbor. Turtle looks up at the vines and says, "bean trees." Taylor follows her eyes to see that the flowers on the wisteria vine have gone to seed, producing green pods that look just like beans. Taylor considers it another miracle that these flowers have turned to beans.

After the trip to the park, Taylor goes into Lee Sing's grocery, where Edna Poppy is shopping. Edna, who is holding a white cane, asks Taylor to tell her if she is holding lemons or limes. With a start, Taylor realizes that Edna is blind. A number of odd facts suddenly make sense to Taylor. Edna always wears red because it makes dressing easier, Virgie Parsons always announces everyone's name when the two walk into a room so Edna will know who is present, and Edna looks over people's heads when she talks to them because she can only look in the general direction of their voices.

Taylor goes to visit Esperanza, who is staying at Mattie's house. During the visit, Esperanza stays quiet, and Taylor chatters, trying to say the right thing. She tells Esperanza she loves her name, which means both hope and wait, and that Esperanza reminds her of Turtle because both understand everything people say even though people forget they are listening. Taylor tells her she is sorry for Esperanza's lost child and that she hopes Esperanza will never give up hope. Toward the end of the conversation, Esperanza begins to cry, and Taylor feels that tears are better than the emptiness that filled Esperanza's eyes when Taylor first arrived. On the way home,

Taylor runs into Lou Ann, who has been out looking for jobs. Lou Ann tells her about an interview for a job at a convenience store, where the man called her "sweetheart" and stared at her breasts. As they walk home, they pass by Fanny Heaven, and Lou Ann expresses her disgust at the strip joint, especially the door handle that pushes into a painting of a woman's crotch. Taylor tells her to stop ignoring the door and "talk back to it."

CHAPTER ELEVEN: DREAM ANGELS

Lou Ann gets a job at the Red Hot Mama's salsa factory, where she puts her heart and soul into her work. Although the factory reminds Taylor of a sweatshop, Lou Ann loves her job and brings home all kinds of salsa and new recipes. Lou Ann stops making disparaging remarks about her own body. She works an evening shift, so Taylor usually puts the children to bed, and then the two women eat a late supper together when Lou Ann gets home. One evening, they talk about Lou Ann's tendency to worry. Lou Ann tells Taylor that she had a dream right after Dwayne Ray was born. In the dream, an angel came to her and told her that Dwayne Ray would not live to see the year 2000. According to Lou Ann, her own and Dwayne Ray's horoscopes supported this premonition. Since then, Lou Ann has been terrified that Dwayne Ray will die. Since girlhood, Lou Ann has feared death. As a child, she and her brother played a game in which they imagined themselves older, but she refused to dream past her teenage years, scared that she would imagine herself dead. Lou Ann recognizes her thoughts as irrational and berates herself, but Taylor tells her that her tendency to worry also makes her a caring, careful person and mother.

Angel sends a box of presents: a hair clip for Lou Ann and a pair of boots for Dwayne Ray. He also sends a letter saying he misses Lou Ann and wants her and Dwayne Ray to come live in his yurt (domed tent) with him. Lou Ann debates what to do. She feels flattered that he misses her, but she cares about her new responsibilities at the factory, where she has been promoted to floor manager. Taylor fears that Lou Ann will go live with Angel. Lou Ann's possible departure and Esperanza and Estevan's troubles upset Taylor. Mattie is worried that Estevan and Esperanza will be deported. In Guatemala, the government would almost certainly assassinate them. They could stay in the U.S. if they could prove their lives were in danger when they left Central America, but they do not have any documents to prove their case.

ANALYSIS — CHAPTERS TEN–ELEVEN

Again, Kingsolver returns to the idea that beauty springs from barren places. When Turtle sees the wisteria flower gone to seed and the long pods falling from the branches, she calls the wisteria "bean trees." The metamorphosis of flowers into beans is nothing less than a miracle to Taylor. New life seems to burgeon in Lou Ann, too. When she and Taylor talk about the birdcalls, Lou Ann insists, over Taylor's objections, that the birdcall sounds like "who cooks for who." Pleased, Taylor thinks that this marks the first time Lou Ann has stuck to her own opinion. As small as this moment seems, it represents the beginnings of change in Lou Ann. She feels more confident and less inclined to bow to the opinions of others. This confidence mounts at the end of the chapter, when she and Taylor pass by Fanny Heaven. The strip club always disgusted Lou Ann, but for the first time she voices her opinions aloud. She also tells Taylor about her annoyance at the leering man who interviewed her while staring at her breasts. For the first time, Lou Ann has an encouraging, spunky woman to listen to her, and in response she begins to speak up.

> Lou Ann shuddered. "That door's what gets me. The way they made the door handle. Like a woman is something you shove on and walk right through. I try to ignore it, but it still gets me."
>
> (See QUOTATIONS, p. 53)

In Chapter Eleven, Lou Ann fully comprehends that Angel has left for good and that she must go on without him and support her family. The fact that she loves the factory where she works despite its unpleasantness suggests that earning money gives Lou Ann a needed sense of purpose. Because of her new job, Lou Ann stops reading disaster stories and criticizing herself. As Taylor says, the job seems to iron out some of Lou Ann's "wrinkled edges." Just as Lou Ann begins to gain self-confidence and self-reliance, however, Angel sends word that he misses her and wants to be with her again. The package he sends indicates his unfamiliarity with his family: the boots are far too big for Dwayne Ray, and Lou Ann's hair is too short for clips.

CHAPTERS TWELVE–THIRTEEN

SUMMARY —CHAPTER TWELVE: INTO THE TERRIBLE NIGHT

> *The sloped desert plain that lay between us and the city was like a palm stretched out for a fortuneteller to read, with its mounds and hillocks, its life lines and heart lines of dry stream beds.*
>
> (See QUOTATIONS, p. 54)

One afternoon in July the cicadas stop buzzing and Taylor and Mattie hear thunder in the distance. Mattie closes up shop and takes Taylor, Esperanza, and Estevan to the desert, saying she wants them to smell the first rain. She tells them that the Native Americans who used to live in the desert celebrated New Year's Day on the day of the first summer rain. The group climbs up to a hill and listens to the thunder. Rain clouds move in, rain drenches them for a moment, and then the storm moves on.

On the walk back to the car, they see a rattlesnake curling up a tree, presumably looking for birds' eggs. When Taylor gets home, she realizes that something is wrong when she sees Lou Ann's face. Lou Ann tells her something has happened to Turtle. Turtle was in the park with Edna Poppy, who was baby-sitting her, when a man attacked Turtle. Because of her blindness, Edna does not know exactly what happened, but she says that she heard struggling and swung her cane in the direction of the noise. Taylor looks at Turtle, whose eyes are as blank as they were when Taylor found her in Oklahoma. Within a few minutes, a policeman and social worker arrive. Taylor excuses herself to help Mrs. Parsons deal with a sparrow that has flown into the house. The bird bangs into the window and falls back on the counter. Mrs. Parsons thinks it is dead, but it gets back up, and eventually Taylor and Mrs. Parsons manage to get it out the door and "into the terrible night."

A medical examiner finds bruises on Turtle's shoulder but no evidence of molestation. Lou Ann wants to take care of Turtle and find the perpetrator; she is angry with Taylor, who chased the bird instead of tending to Turtle. After the incident, Taylor feels absolutely despondent. She avoids eating and spends most of her time at work.

SUMMARY — CHAPTER THIRTEEN:
NIGHT-BLOOMING CEREUS

Taylor and Turtle meet twice a week with Cynthia, a social worker whose prim professionalism sometimes irks Taylor. Eventually, Cynthia finds out about Turtle's past and tells Taylor that Taylor has no legal claim to the child. Without a legal guardian, Turtle is a ward of the state. Lou Ann, outraged by this information, tries to persuade Taylor to find some way around the law. Taylor feels hopeless and depressed, and seems ready to give up any effort to keep Turtle. Lou Ann laments the change in the once-gutsy Taylor.

Mattie has not found a way to get Esperanza and Estevan out of the state and into another sanctuary. She reminisces with Taylor about their first meeting, telling the surprised Taylor that she saw through Taylor's show of confidence on that first day, when Taylor struck her as a "bewildered parent." Mattie tries to tell her now that no parent can offer a child a perfect upbringing and that the only question Taylor must ask herself is whether she wants to do the best she can for Turtle.

Taylor makes an appointment to talk to Cynthia about Turtle's custody. Taylor asks if laws regarding custody are different on Indian reservations, and how she should go about finding out about how laws differ in other states. Over the course of the conversation, Taylor realizes that Cynthia is on her side and wants Taylor to keep Turtle. Cynthia helps Taylor by giving her the number of someone in Oklahoma who could give her legal advice. After a sleepless night, Taylor decides she will drive to Oklahoma to take Esperanza and Estevan to a sanctuary and look for Turtle's relatives. Lou Ann worries that Turtle's relatives might want her back or that Taylor might not be able to find them, but she forgets the greatest risk: that Taylor could be caught transporting illegal immigrants. The wise and practical Mattie, on the other hand, realizes that Taylor has agreed to place herself in great danger. The night before Taylor leaves, Virgie Parsons invites Lou Ann, Taylor, and the children over to their porch to see the cereus. The cereus, which blooms just once a year, and only at night, has burst into blossoms. The plant's flowers float above the women's heads and smell wonderful. It seems like a good omen.

Taylor, Turtle, Esperanza, and Estevan leave from Mattie's. Mattie reassures Taylor but seems nervous. She implies that Taylor is a hero for risking her own safety, and she looks at Taylor as Alice, Taylor's mother, used to. Once on the road, they pass a dead blackbird. Taylor thinks to brake but realizes that stopping for a dead bird does not do any good.

ANALYSIS — CHAPTERS THIRTEEN–FOURTEEN

Kingsolver links the beauty of the land to Native American values, suggesting that Native Americans have an admirable appreciation for the natural world. The characters pay homage to Native American tradition when they experience the magical first rain. Taylor's growing knowledge of the land and the natural world reflects her growing understanding of Native American identity. Her delight at the rain also reflects the novel's major theme: joy results from finding beauty in the midst of ugliness. In Chapter Twelve, the rain explodes onto the barren desert, thrilling the onlookers.

The two stories in Chapter Twelve, the story of the rain and the story of Turtle's attack, are linked by the snake. After the rain ends, the group sees a snake trying to find birds' eggs. This encounter foreshadows their discovery that Turtle, who is often associated with birds, has been attacked by an evil man, represented by the snake. The literal snake-and-bird encounter becomes metaphoric, as a silent assailant attacks the birdlike Turtle. Kingsolver employs more bird symbolism at the end of the chapter, when a bird gets caught inside the house. The plight of the panicky, trapped bird symbolizes Turtle's trauma. Taylor stresses the connection between the bird and Turtle when she confuses the two situations, thinking that the terrible event everyone is talking about concerns the trapped bird, when they are actually talking about Turtle. The fact that the bird appears dead echoes Turtle's reversion into a nearly catatonic state. Simultaneously, however, the nearly dead appearance of the bird is hopeful, since the bird survives and goes back into the "terrible night." Taylor demonstrates both the depth of her love for Turtle and the persistence of her immaturity. The attack on Turtle clearly disturbs her—she sinks into a depression because of it—but she also pulls away from Turtle in Turtle's hour of need. She is inexperienced, feeling that because she cannot prevent bad things from happening to Turtle, she is not a good mother.

In these chapters, the usually feisty Taylor becomes depressed, and the usually meek Lou Ann becomes bold. As Taylor learns more about mothering and the injustices of the world, she becomes less sure of herself and more disillusioned with the world. When she remembers her show of bravery in front of Mattie, she realizes she feels too tired and old to feign bravery anymore. Taylor's grit seems to have rubbed off on Lou Ann, however, so that when Taylor has to face hardship, Lou Ann toughens her up, fighting on Turtle's behalf and scolding Taylor for her lassitude. Kingsolver creates a community of women characters who continually bolster each other. When Lou Ann and Taylor support one another in the midst of their role reversal, they illustrate the usefulness of female friendship. Mattie supports Taylor too; talking to Mattie is what begins to pull Taylor out of her depression. Taylor has felt like a failed mother, but Mattie comforts her by explaining that no parent can hope to protect her child from the world. This assurance heartens Taylor, and she regains her energy, deciding to go to Oklahoma to save Estevan and Esperanza and do all she can to keep Turtle.

CHAPTERS FOURTEEN–FIFTEEN

SUMMARY—CHAPTER FOURTEEN: GUARDIAN SAINTS

Taylor, Esperanza, Estevan, and Turtle drive east toward Oklahoma. They must pass through a routine Immigration check in New Mexico. Because she is so nervous, Taylor hesitates when the officer asks who Turtle's parents are. Estevan indicates that Turtle belongs to him and his wife. Taylor agrees with him that this tactic was best, but she feels a little hurt, as she does later when Turtle begins calling Esperanza "Ma." Estevan tells Taylor that he and Esperanza are not Guatemalan but Mayan, and that their real names are Indian. Taylor marvels at the number of languages they speak. She recalls a moment when Esperanza showed her the St. Christopher medallion around her neck. St. Christopher is the guardian saint of refugees, and Taylor thinks that Stephen Foster, who wrote Kentucky's state song, looks a little like the guardian saint.

Esperanza amuses Turtle in the backseat, singing to her while Estevan and Taylor talk in the front seat. Finally, the group arrives in Oklahoma, stopping at the Broken Arrow Motor Lodge, where Taylor stayed with Turtle. The owner, Mrs. Hoge, has died. Although Taylor offers to take Estevan and Esperanza to their new home right away, they want to stay with Taylor while she looks for Turtle's relatives. In the car, Taylor overhears Esperanza call Turtle Ismene, and begins to worry. She misses Lou Ann. When Taylor locates the bar where the Indian woman gave Turtle to her, she finds that it has changed hands, and the current owners know nothing of

Turtle's relatives. The group eats lunch at the bar and before they leave, the girl working there tells Taylor that the Cherokee nation is not barren at all; she says most of it exists in the Ozark Mountains, which is filled with beautiful lakes. Taylor feels she owes her great grandfather an apology for misjudging the Cherokee Nation. Frustrated in her attempt to find Turtle's relatives, Taylor begins to feel like she has come a long way for no reason. She asks Esperanza and Estevan if they'd like to go to the Lake o' the Cherokees, a lake in the Ozarks, for a vacation, and they decide to go.

Summary—Chapter Fifteen: Lake o' the Cherokees

As the group drives to the lake in the Cherokee Nation, Taylor, the only white person in the group, begins to feel like the odd one out. She notices marked changes in Estevan and Esperanza, who seem relaxed in this place where everyone looks like them. Taylor is happy to find she was wrong to assume that the Cherokee Nation is desolate—the place of her head rights is actually lush and mountainous. On the way to the lake, Taylor gets worried when Turtle looks out the window and shouts "Mama." There is no woman in sight, just a gas station and a cemetery.

At the lake the group finds a cottage to stay in for a night. They spend the afternoon next to a stream, where Estevan picks flowers for Esperanza and Taylor. Taylor notes something in Esperanza "thawing"; Esperanza seems happy for the first time. In the afternoon, Estevan and Taylor rent a boat and go out on the lake. Thinking of Estevan's imminent departure, Taylor cries. She tells him she will miss him. He does not say he will miss her, and Taylor realizes they are treading on dangerous ground. Estevan suggests that they make a wish. Instead of coins, they throw beer pop-tops into the lake, which Estevan calls "appropriate for American wishes." Taylor makes two wishes, only one of which she can hope for. The implication is that Taylor wishes to keep Estevan and Turtle, although she can only truly hope to keep the girl.

Back at the shore, the group has a picnic lunch. Turtle buries her doll underneath a tree. Taylor begins to explain to her that while seeds grow, dolls do not. When Turtle looks at the pile of dirt and says "Mama," Taylor understands that Taylor is remembering her biological mother's burial and reenacting it with her doll. She tells Turtle it is terrible to lose your mother and asks Turtle if she knows her mother is gone forever. She tells Turtle she will try her best to keep Turtle forever. Turtle seems to understand. At the end of the chapter, Taylor asks Esperanza and Estevan if they will do her a favor, and they agree.

ANALYSIS—CHAPTERS FOURTEEN–FIFTEEN

The revelation that Esperanza and Estevan are descendants of the ancient Mayans changes the way Taylor sees their relationship with Turtle, because Turtle's race, cultural history, and appearance make her a natural fit with Esperanza and Estevan, not with Taylor. Taylor feels hurt when she hears Esperanza singing to Turtle in Esperanza's native language and when Estevan tells the immigration official that Turtle belongs to him. Not only does Turtle look like Estevan and Esperanza, but she also fills the hole left in their family by the disappearance of Ismene. Like them, too, Turtle can claim no permanent home. Estevan says he can no longer remember which place he misses most, for as a Mayan he has had multiple homes but does not really belong anywhere.

The St. Christopher medallion, which symbolizes hope for refugees, provides a small link between Taylor and Esperanza and Estevan. Taylor muses that the saint looks like Stephen Foster, the man who wrote the Kentucky state song, an association that suggests Taylor's identification as a refugee. Just as Esperanza has St. Christopher, Taylor has Stephen Foster. Although her separation from home was neither forced nor severely disruptive, she nevertheless feels that she does not truly belong anywhere. She did not belong in Kentucky, and Arizona seems to be a temporary home. Everyone begins to feel more at home upon reaching the Cherokee Nation. Estevan and Esperanza feel relief at finding a place where people look like them, and Taylor seems to agree with the girl in the bar who defines the Cherokee Nation as a people, not a place. Taylor's home has more to do with her daughter than with geography.

Turtle symbolically buries her past life when she buries her doll. Kingsolver implies that the circumstances surrounding Turtle's mother's death and burial were terrifying, and here Turtle reenacts the scene not with a feeling of terror, but one of calm control. She feels herself safe with Taylor, and she orchestrates a peaceful burial for her doll, a stand-in for her mother. This cathartic burial, possible only in Turtle's homeland, suggests that she now belongs more fully to Taylor.

Chapters Sixteen–Seventeen

Summary — Chapter Sixteen:
Soundness of Mind and Freedom of Will

Estevan, Esperanza, Taylor, and Turtle go to the office of Mr. Jonas Wilford Armistead. Estevan and Esperanza pose as Steve and Hope and say they are Turtle's biological parents. Taylor poses as Turtle's adoptive mother. Mr. Armistead, who assumes they are telling the truth, explains the permanence of the adoption, and asks Estevan and Esperanza to confirm they can give up their child. Esperanza begins to cry, and Taylor realizes that she is not acting. Esperanza says they love their daughter but cannot care for her. She says that someday, when they have a home, they might have more children. Watching Esperanza hold Turtle, Taylor realizes that if Esperanza said she wanted to keep Turtle, Taylor could not deny her. However, Esperanza gives her St. Christopher medallion to Turtle and tells Taylor she knows Turtle will grow up happy. Estevan and Esperanza sign a document stating that they agree to the change in custody and that they sign in "soundness of mind and freedom of will." Afterward, Esperanza's face seems newly happy.

Summary — Chapter Seventeen: Rhizobia

> [Turtle] . . . entertained me with her vegetable-soup song, except that now there were people mixed in with the beans and potatoes: Dwayne Ray, Mattie, Esperanza, Lou Ann and all the rest. And me. I was the main ingredient.　　(See QUOTATIONS, p. 55)

Taylor takes Estevan and Esperanza to the church where the reverend and his wife will provide them with shelter. Taylor must say goodbye to Estevan. She tells him she has never before lost anyone she loves. When she asks if it will be safe to write, he tells her he can only send messages through Mattie. He kisses her before he goes into the house, and Taylor muses, "[A]ll four of us had buried someone we loved in Oklahoma." After leaving Estevan and Esperanza, Taylor calls her mother from a pay phone and tells her she lost her love. Alice comforts her. She tells Taylor that she has quit her job cleaning houses, and Taylor tells her about Turtle's official adoption. Taylor and Turtle have their "second real conversation" (the first concerned Turtle's burial of her doll). When Turtle says she would like to see "Ma Woo-Ahn," Taylor explains that although Turtle has many friends, she now has only one Ma in the world. She tells Turtle her name is now April Turtle Greer.

On a whim, Taylor decides to call 1-800-THE-LORD, a number she imagined calling if she ever hit rock bottom, just as her mother imagined cashing in their head rights in the Cherokee Nation. When she calls, the number turns out to be a pledge line. Taylor is not disappointed, but amused, and she tells the woman who answers that the number has been a "fountain of faith" for her. She and Turtle go to a library, where they look at horticulture reference books. Turtle sees a picture of wisteria and recognizes it as bean trees. Taylor reads out loud about wisteria vines, which grow with the help of rhizobia, microscopic bugs that suck nitrogen from the soil to help the plant. Taylor explains that the bugs are like an underground railroad helping the plant, just as people have people helping them. Taylor takes Turtle to the courthouse to pick up the adoption papers, and calls Lou Ann. She nervously asks Lou Ann if she plans to go back to Angel, and Lou Ann emphatically says no. Lou Ann tells Taylor about a new man she is dating, a former Rastafarian with a dog named Mr. T. She says that she does not plan to move in with this man, because she feels like Taylor and Turtle are her family. Taylor tells Lou Ann that she has adopted Turtle, to Lou Ann's great relief. Finally, Taylor and Turtle leave Oklahoma City, heading back to Tucson. Turtle sings what Taylor calls her "vegetable-soup song." Along with vegetable names, Turtle adds the names of her friends—Lou Ann, Esperanza, Mattie, Dwayne Ray, and Taylor, "the main ingredient."

ANALYSIS — CHAPTERS SIXTEEN–SEVENTEEN

Just as Turtle closed a chapter in her life by reenacting the burial of her mother, Esperanza finds relief in the ceremony of giving up Turtle. Esperanza never got a chance to say goodbye to her daughter, Ismene, so she finds closure in a formal goodbye scene with a girl who looks like her own child and whom she loves like her own child. She also has the comforting illusion that she has left her own daughter in good hands with Taylor, a relief because she does not know who now cares for Ismene. The goodbye serves as a catharsis, a purification leading to renewal. Taylor notices that Esperanza's face looks refreshed as she leaves the office. As Taylor later tells

Estevan, "[S]he seems . . . as happy as if she'd really found a place to leave Ismene behind."

Taylor says that "all four of us had buried someone we loved in Oklahoma"; Turtle buries her biological mother, Esperanza buries Ismene, and Taylor buries Estevan. Taylor does not explain whether the person Estevan loves and buries is herself or Ismene. Taylor and Estevan never express their feelings for each other, but Kingsolver implies that each understands Taylor's love for Estevan and his acknowledgement that in different circumstances, they could have been together. In the moral world of this novel, Taylor and Estevan cannot run off with each other, or even sleep with each other, for several reasons: Estevan, a good man, loves and respects his wife; Taylor does not want to betray Esperanza; and although the novel prizes all-female families, it also respects conventional families such as Estevan and Esperanza's and does not advocate shattering them.

Taylor's successful maturation is confirmed when, in Chapter Seventeen, she realizes she no longer needs her ace in the hole, 1-800-THE-LORD. She has hit her low point and lived through it, and she now feels strong and happy. She says that 1-800-THE-LORD used to be her "fountain of faith"; the number turns out to be a sham, but Taylor now recognizes that her friends provide her with a true fountain of faith. Kingsolver contrasts the useless phone call Taylor makes to 1-800-THE-LORD with the reviving, helpful phone calls she makes to her mother and Lou Ann. Taylor also demonstrates the fullness of her maturation by identifying herself to Turtle, for the first time, as Turtle's mother. Taylor now feels eager to provide care and love for her child.

IMPORTANT QUOTATIONS EXPLAINED

1. "I have always thought you had a wonderful way with words," he said. "You don't need to go fishing for big words in the dictionary. You are poetic, mi'ija." . . . "Well, thank you for the compliment," I said, "but that's the biggest bunch of hogwash, what you said. When did I ever say anything poetic?" "Washing hogs is poetic," he said.

These lines from Chapter Eight record a conversation between Estevan and Taylor. To emphasize the idea that immigrants should be treated with respect, Kingsolver pointedly makes Estevan, an immigrant, the character with the best command of the English language. He is better educated and more articulate than any of his friends, all of whom use slang and bad grammar. Kingsolver does not condemn those characters who use nonstandard English, as this quotation indicates; rather, she suggests that all forms of English can be considered poetic. Although Taylor wishes she could use bigger words, like Estevan does, Estevan points out that her slang and colloquial expressions are beautiful. Taylor's "hogwash," Esperanza's silence, and Turtle's vegetable songs all have their own bit of poetry.

2. Turtle shook her head. "Bean trees," she said, as plainly as if she had been thinking about it all day. We looked where she was pointing. Some of the wisteria flowers had gone to seed, and all these wonderful long green pods hung down from the branches. They looked as much like beans as anything you'd ever care to eat. "Will you look at that," I said. It was another miracle. The flower trees were turning into bean trees.

These lines, which come from Chapter Ten, occur as Lou Ann, Taylor, Turtle, and Dwayne Ray sit in Roosevelt Park (commonly known as "Dog Doo Park"). The quotation points to the novel's idea that miracles happen in modest or unlikely places. Appropriately, it is Turtle who makes the discovery that gives the novel its title. Turtle is herself a miracle in an unlikely place. Like the bean trees discovered in the ugly park, Turtle is discovered in a barren parking lot. And like the dirty, barren park, which later seems magical, Turtle at first strikes Taylor as an unwanted burden, but gradually becomes more and more important to Taylor, until the possibility of losing Turtle becomes the main conflict in the novel.

3.   Lou Ann shuddered. "That door's what gets me. The
      way they made the door handle. Like a woman is
      something you shove on and walk right through. I try
      to ignore it, but it still gets me." "Don't ignore it,
      then," I said. "Talk back to it. Say, 'You can't do that
      number on me, you shit-for-brains.' . . . What I'm
      saying is you can't just sit there, you got to get
      pissed off."

In Chapter Ten, Lou Ann and Taylor discuss Fanny Heaven, the
local strip joint. Lou Ann has just had her first job interview, during
which her interviewer talked to her breasts instead of to her face.
This quotation demonstrates Taylor's usual feistiness and spirited
support of her friend. With Taylor, Lou Ann feels comfortable artic-
ulating a disgust that until this point she kept secret. Previously, Lou
Ann had tolerated the offensive strip club in silence, thinking of it as
an unassailable part of her surroundings. Here, for the first time, she
identifies her discomfort aloud, even identifying what particularly
upsets her: the mural of a woman painted so that the door handle
opens into the woman's crotch. Kingsolver makes a point by including Fanny Heaven in her novel. The existence of the strip club suggests that the sexual violence or violent attacks suffered by women
do not spring from nowhere, but are the byproduct of a society that
objectifies and exploits women's bodies.

QUOTATIONS

4. The whole Tucson Valley lay in front of us, resting in its cradle of mountains. The sloped desert plain that lay between us and the city was like a palm stretched out for a fortuneteller to read, with its mounds and hillocks, its life lines and heart lines of dry stream beds.

This description comes in Chapter Twelve, at the time of the first rain, when Mattie takes her young friends into the desert so they can see the natural world come to life. This quotation, typical of Kingsolver's descriptions of the natural landscape, shows her consciousness of the environment. It also exemplifies Kingsolver's use of unusual metaphors. By describing the landscape as the palm of a human hand, Kingsolver personifies the mountains and city. Her phrase "resting in its cradle of mountains" likens the valley to a baby, and the phrases "city like a palm" and "life lines and heart lines" suggest an adult. The land embodies a life lived from birth to death. Taylor falls in love with the Arizona land and sky, and her appreciation for nature in all its forms, with all its surprises, mirrors the values the novel espouses.

5. It didn't seem to matter to Turtle, she was happy
   where she was. . . . She watched the dark highway and
   entertained me with her vegetable-soup song, except
   that now there were people mixed in with the beans
   and potatoes: Dwayne Ray, Mattie, Esperanza,
   Lou Ann and all the rest. And me. I was the
   main ingredient.

These lines recount Taylor's thoughts at the end of the novel, in Chapter Seventeen, as she and Turtle head back to Tucson. With this final scene, Kingsolver provides a mirror image of Taylor's first trip to Tucson with Turtle, during which the little girl's behavior was entirely different. On the first trip, Turtle remained so silent and motionless that Turtle wondered if she had died. On this trip, Turtle remains wide awake, happily babbling about her vegetables. Most important, Turtle now includes names of people in her vegetable-soup song. This marks a change, because in the beginning, Turtle could not connect with people or form ties to them. By adding names of people she knows to her babble, Turtle shows she has begun to recover from her history of abuse and has gained the ability to trust people. Most significant is that she identifies Taylor as the "main ingredient." For a space of time, Turtle demonstrated her confusion about her caretakers by calling most women in her life "Ma." Now, she identifies Taylor as her mother. The last sentence of this quotation reaffirms not only Turtle's attachment to Taylor, but also Taylor's happiness in hearing herself identified as the main ingredient, and her confidence in herself as a mother.

QUOTATIONS

KEY FACTS

FULL TITLE
: *The Bean Trees*

AUTHOR
: Barbara Kingsolver

TYPE OF WORK
: Novel

GENRE
: Journey or quest novel

LANGUAGE
: English

TIME AND PLACE WRITTEN
: Tucson, Arizona; 1986–1987

DATE OF FIRST PUBLICATION
: 1988

PUBLISHER
: HarperCollins

NARRATOR
: Most of the chapters are narrated by Taylor Greer, but Chapters Two and Four, which introduce Lou Ann, are narrated by an anonymous, omniscient narrator

POINT OF VIEW
: For the most part, the story is told from Taylor's point of view, and we are privy to her thoughts and feelings. Chapters Two and Four are written from a limited omniscient perspective, from which the narrator explains Lou Ann's thinking.

TONE
: Folksy, poetic, humorous

TENSE
: Immediate past

SETTING (TIME)
: Early 1980s

SETTING (PLACE)

The novel opens in rural Kentucky. Taylor travels across the country to Tucson, Arizona, where she settles. At the end of the novel, she takes a trip to Oklahoma before returning to Tucson.

PROTAGONIST

Taylor Greer

MAJOR CONFLICT

Taylor tries to accept the responsibility of caring for another person and to understand the plight of political refugees

RISING ACTION

Taylor receives Taylor, grows close to Mattie and Lou Ann, and learns the story of Estevan and Esperanza

CLIMAX

Taylor decides to fight to keep Turtle and to risk her own safety for Estevan and Esperanza

FALLING ACTION

Estevan and Esperanza pretend to be Turtle's biological parents so that Taylor may adopt the little girl legally; Taylor delivers Estevan and Esperanza to their new home; Taylor and Turtle head back home to Tucson.

THEMES

The shared burden of womanhood; the plight of illegal immigrants; respect for the environment

MOTIFS

Rebirth; motherhood

SYMBOLS

Beans and bean trees; Ismene; birds

FORESHADOWING

The postcard with two Indian women on it, which Taylor sends to her mother, foreshadows Taylor and Turtle's relationship. The snake in the desert foreshadows the prowler that attacks Turtle. The survival of the bird that is trapped in the house foreshadows Turtle's recovery.

KEY FACTS

STUDY QUESTIONS &
ESSAY TOPICS

STUDY QUESTIONS

1. *Traditionally, American society has defined "family" as "nuclear family"—a father, a mother, and children living together. The biological mother is often viewed as the natural caregiver, and the father is viewed as the provider. How does this novel ask us to rethink our definition of family and how does it suggest alternative role models in place of or in addition to the biological mother?*

This novel presents several models of unconventional yet functional families. Kingsolver does not scoff at the traditional family Taylor affectionately refers to a family of paper dolls she had as a child. She remembers loving the dolls and intensely longing for a family like theirs. Kingsolver suggests such perfect doll families exist less and less frequently, and women must come up with new versions of family. Lou Ann and Taylor form a new familial structure that does not depend on a romantic or a blood relationship, but still provides two parental figures for the children. At the end of the novel, Lou Ann responds to the news of Turtle's adoption with a relief and joy that rivals Taylor's. This novel values a sociopolitical system that regards caregiving as the work of a community, not an individual.

The first mother introduced in the novel, Alice Greer, sets the stage for all the models of motherhood to come. Alice is a loving, responsible single mother, and her daughter does not grieve the absence of a male role model—in fact, she counts herself lucky to lack a father in a town where men call their daughters sluts, or get girls pregnant and run away. As the novel progresses, Kingsolver presents more models of motherhood: Taylor becomes an adoptive mother overnight, acquiring a child of a different racial makeup and background than her own. Lou Ann gives birth to a child on her own. We never find out if Mattie has children of her own or not, but this seems unimportant. Mattie provides for many "adopted" people, loving them and risking her safety for them just as a mother would.

2.   *What is the relationship between religion and spirituality
       in this novel? What role do the conspicuous signs of
       commercialized religious belief (Jesus Is Lord Used Tires
       and the sign reading 1-800-THE LORD) play in
       establishing the novel's moral code?*

The Bean Trees reverberates with a deep sense of spirituality that
has little to do with organized religion. In the novel, commercialized
religion works not as the means to salvation, but as a humorous
lucky charm. At the bar with the sign that reads 1-800-THE-LORD,
Taylor finds Turtle, who will become the most precious part of her
life. Jesus Is Lord Used Tires brings Taylor to Mattie, who becomes
a mother figure and mentor. While the Jesus mural on the wall of the
used-tire store holds no sacred value for Lou Ann and Taylor, they
relish the fact that it scares off would-be patrons of the neighboring
strip club.

3.   To *what extent does the novel define home in terms of geographic setting? In terms of people?*

Kingsolver first addresses the question of home as geographic setting when Taylor reaches Oklahoma. Taylor thinks back to the way her mother talked about the Cherokee Nation, and feels thoroughly let down. Still, although her mother's Cherokee "head rights" do not amount to much, she finds head rights of her own when an Indian woman gives her Turtle. The postcard Taylor writes to her mother indicates that Taylor's obligation is to a little girl, not to a geographic place: "I found my head rights, Mama. They're coming with me." Taylor's sense of home has to do not with the geographical location of the Cherokee nation, but with Turtle.

Eventually, Taylor does locate a physical place that feels like home. The quirky beauty of the Arizona desert begins to feel homey, and by the time she returns to Tucson at the end of the novel, she is returning both to her geographic home, and to her home community of people. Esperanza and Estevan are forced to define home as the place where they have friends, rather than as the location of their homeland. When they arrive at the Cherokee Nation, where they look similar to the inhabitants, they seem heartened. Although they cannot live in their native South America, they find a community of similarly displaced people where they blend in. As someone tells Taylor, the Cherokee Nation is not a place, but a people.

SUGGESTED ESSAY TOPICS

1. Questions of legality surface many times in this novel. How does the novel regard the law? If the law cannot act as an authority, what dictates right and wrong in its place?

2. Compare the experiences of Esperanza and Estevan, who are of the Mayan people, to the experiences of Turtle, and the Cherokee people in general.

3. Think of the bird imagery in this novel. What do the birds symbolize? How are different kinds of birds used to represent different ideas?

4. *The Bean Trees* is a novel about refugees. Identify the characters in the novel who have left or been driven from their homelands. What differentiates their experiences, and what commonalities bind them together?

5. What is the significance of the many different forms of violence referred to in this novel?

REVIEW & RESOURCES

QUIZ

1. How does Taylor spend the money she earns working at the hospital?

   A. She buys ten hogs
   B. She buys a present for Turtle
   C. She buys a Volkswagon bug
   D. She buys a new dress for her mother

2. How does Taylor acquire Turtle?

   A. She finds her at Lou Ann's house
   B. A woman gives Turtle to Taylor
   C. She adopts her through an agency
   D. She takes her from Esperanza

3. What bird symbolizes Turtle?

   A. The bird that makes its home in a cactus
   B. The quail
   C. The bird that gets trapped in the house
   D. All of the above

4. How do people eat in heaven, according to Estevan?

   A. With their hands
   B. With their eyes
   C. Accompanied by children
   D. By feeding each other with long spoons

5. Why does Mattie take her friends into the desert one evening in July?

   A.   So that they can smell the rain
   B.   To show them Tucson's city limits from afar
   C.   Because she thinks that they should see a snake
   D.   To prove to them that the desert is a dry, lifeless place

6. What signals Lou Ann's growing sense of independence and confidence?

   A. She gets a job at the Red Hot Mama's salsa factory
   B. She stops comparing herself to a farm animal
   C. She refuses to take Angel back
   D. All of the above

7. Why was Turtle vulnerable to the prowler in the park?

   A. She is not shy
   B. She is not very smart
   C. Edna Poppy, her baby-sitter, is blind
   D. Dwayne Ray was distracting her

8. What do Taylor and Estevan toss into the Lake o' the Cherokees when they make their wishes?

   A. Pennies
   B. Dolls
   C. Their rings
   D. Beer pop-tops

9. What does Mattie have in her garden besides vegetables and flowers?

   A. A statue of Elvis
   B. A statue of Jesus
   C. Car tires
   D. A fountain

10. Of whom does Mattie remind Taylor?

    A. Newt Hardbine
    B. The Virgin Mary
    C. One of the girls at Fannie Heaven
    D. Alice Greer

11. How does Turtle get her name?

    A. She is slow at everything
    B. She has a firm grip
    C. She hides behind things
    D. She is fond of the tortoises at the zoo

12. What happens that causes Turtle to mutter her first sound?

    A. Taylor tickles her
    B. The car has to stop suddenly for a family of quail
    C. Dwayne Ray takes her Old McDonald book
    D. Mattie brings her apple juice

13. How does Sandi from Burger Derby afford baby-sitting for her child?

    A. She takes advantage of the mall's free day care
    B. The Burger Derby pays her well
    C. Taylor gives her some money
    D. She leaves her child with Mattie

14. What are Alice Greer's "head rights"?

    A. An expensive salon hairdo
    B. 1-800-THE-LORD
    C. Taylor's Volkswagon bug
    D. Her Cherokee blood

15. What does Taylor identify as a reason she would have to give up Turtle?

    A. Turtle wetting her pants
    B. Turtle burying her doll
    C. Esperanza asking if she could keep Turtle
    D. Finding no honest way of obtaining adoption papers

16. Who could be seen as Turtle's tragic counterpart?

    A. Ismene
    B. Dwayne Ray
    C. Taylor as a young girl
    D. Newt Hardbine

17. What's in the bottle that Granny Logan takes to Lou Ann?

    A. Sand
    B. Tug Fork water
    C. Poison to kill Angel
    D. Evian

18. What does Taylor avoid all through her years in Kentucky?

    A. Hospitals
    B. School
    C. Her mother
    D. Getting pregnant

19. Where does Lou Ann end up working?

    A. At the rodeo
    B. At a salsa factory
    C. At Fanny Heaven
    D. At Jesus Is Lord Used Tires

20. Of the following, who to the reader's knowledge still goes by his or her original name?

    A. Estevan
    B. Lou Ann
    C. Turtle
    D. Taylor

21. What allows Turtle's successful adoption?

    A. The man at the bar gives Taylor his consent
    B. Esperanza takes her and goes back to Guatemala
    C. Taylor leaves her on Mattie's doorstep
    D. Estevan and Esperanza pretend to be her biological parents

22. Who is the patron saint of refugees?

    A. St. Shirley
    B. St. Christopher
    C. St. Stephen
    D. St. Theresa

23. What does Taylor's mother require of her before she leaves Kentucky?

    A. She has to clean the house
    B. She has to sit up on the Chevron sign
    C. She has to learn about auto maintenance
    D. She has to explain why she wants to leave

24. To what does Mattie compare her house?

    A. A bird sanctuary
    B. The kingdom of God
    C. A junkyard
    D. A zoo

25. Who, at the end of the novel, is Turtle's "main ingredient" in her vegetable-soup song?

    A. Esperanza
    B. Taylor
    C. St. Christopher
    D. Ismene

SUGGESTIONS FOR FURTHER READING

KINGSOLVER, BARBARA. *Animal Dreams.* New York: HarperPerennial, 1991.

———. *High Tide in Tucson: Essays from Now or Never.* New York: HarperCollins Publishers, 1995.

———. *Pigs in Heaven.* New York: HarperCollins Publishers, 1993.

DEMARR, MARY JEAN. *Barbara Kingsolver: A Critical Companion.* Westport, Connecticut: Greenwood Press, 1999.

GERSHTEN, DONNA M. *Kissing the Virgin's Mouth.* New York: HarperCollins Publishers, 2001.

SLOVIC, SCOTT, ed. *Getting over the Color Green: Contemporary Environmental Literature of the Southwest.* Tucson, Arizona: University of Arizona Press, 2001.

WILDER, KATHRYN, ed. *Walking the Twilight: Women Writers of the Southwest.* Flagstaff, Arizona: Northland Publishing, 1994.

A Note on the Type

The typeface used in SparkNotes study guides is Sabon, created by master typographer Jan Tschichold in 1964. Tschichold revolutionized the field of graphic design twice: first with his use of asymmetrical layouts and sanserif type in the 1930s when he was affiliated with the Bauhaus, then by abandoning assymetry and calling for a return to the classic ideals of design. Sabon, his only extant typeface, is emblematic of his latter program: Tschichold's design is a recreation of the types made by Claude Garamond, the great French typographer of the Renaissance, and his contemporary Robert Granjon. Fittingly, it is named for Garamond's apprentice, Jacques Sabon.

SPARKNOTES
TEST PREPARATION
GUIDES

The SparkNotes team figured it was time to cut standardized tests down to size. We've studied the tests for you, so that SparkNotes test prep guides are:

Smarter:
Packed with critical-thinking skills and test-
taking strategies that will improve your score.

Better:
Fully up to date, covering all new features of the tests,
with study tips on every type of question.

Faster:
Our books cover exactly what you need to
know for the test. No more, no less.

SparkNotes Guide to the SAT & PSAT
SparkNotes Guide to the SAT & PSAT—Deluxe Internet Edition
SparkNotes Guide to the ACT
SparkNotes Guide to the ACT—Deluxe Internet Edition
SparkNotes Guide to the SAT II Writing
SparkNotes Guide to the SAT II U.S. History
SparkNotes Guide to the SAT II Math Ic
SparkNotes Guide to the SAT II Math IIc
SparkNotes Guide to the SAT II Biology
SparkNotes Guide to the SAT II Physics

SparkNotes Study Guides: